WHAT'S YOUR **SALES STORY?**

… of not letting your ego get in the way of your sales success!

Ja Marr Brown

Published by
The Kaizen Way

FIRST EDITION PUBLISHED 2008

ISBN 978-0-9820528-0-8

Cover design / Everywhere Marketing

Printed and bound by Central Plains Book
(*a division of Sun Graphics, LLC.*)

Publisher:

The Kaizen Way
160 W. Foothill Pkwy, 105 # 110
Corona, CA 92882
www.whatsyoursalesstory.com

Special Quantity Discounts:
This book is available at special quantity discounts to use
as premiums, sales promotions, or for use in corporate
training programs. For more information on how to purchase
bulk quantities for your organization please contact us at
info@whatsyoursalesstory.com or 951-737-5579.

"Ja Marr Brown provides today's sales professionals with the real value proposition. I'm not referring to the mechanical nature of selling, but the heart and brain of sales-life and work experiences. Through Ja Marr's personal story and the lessons he has placed in this book you will gain the courage and discipline to look deeply into the most important element of sales success - YOU!"

— **Rob Seguin, President**
The Productive Leadership Institute

"As a trainer and a former sales person myself, the quest for new and breakthrough tools to manage and coach a person to achieve their fullest potential has alluded me...until now. Ja Marr Brown has uncovered a technique that has been sorely missing in the sales training industry. It was through surrendering myself to the process and uncovering my own personal "story" that I believe Ja Marr has uncovered the missing link for higher achievement for anyone willing to do the work."

— **Laura Spaulding, District Sales Manager**
Allergan

"WOW! Finally a book on sales that cuts through the b.s. and tells it like it is. *What's Your Sales Story?* delivers a healthy dose of reality as Ja Marr gets to the very heart of what it takes and means to be a perennial sales performer. I am truly impressed by the depth of which Ja Marr went to reveal his personal setbacks and triumphs as a sales professional. And equally impressed that he wove those experiences into easy to follow exercises readers can use to apply the lessons to their career. Simply put, *What's Your Sales Story?* takes the guesswork out of achieving consistent success in sales."

— **Pete Nelson,CEO**
Everywhere Marketing & Creator of Selling In Color

"Finally! A book that teaches and motivates with words that are transparent and easy to follow."

— **Glen March, MD, Chairman and CEO**
March Vision Care, Inc.

"*What's Your Sales Story?* is one of the most insightful books you'll ever read on sales. Ja Marr Brown has uncovered a unique and highly effective way to increase sales through changing perspective. This book is a must-read for anyone hoping to improve their sales and fast track their career."

— **Sarah Taylor, Author**
Secrets of Successful Pharmaceutical Salespeople

"*What's Your Sales Story?* takes a candid and rarely seen look into what many sales people experience in their development as sales professionals. No career is a breeze, especially when it comes to sales. With this book, however, Ja Marr gives everybody hope and an easy to follow guideline through reflection of how to persevere and develop as a sales person. *What's Your Sales Story?* will accelerate anyone's career performance towards greater results."

— **Alex Lopez, VP of Operations**
Atlantis Eyecare

FOREWORD

Go to any bookstore, and you will encounter shelves or advertorials advising you on the art of self-motivation and how to be a more effective sales person or communicator. The skills they teach and the manner in which they communicate ranges from learned academic to the perspective of the individual in the corner-office or to the wanna-be, stand-up comedian. In their own way, they all have a message to impart, but how will it affect you? One of the tests as to how good these books are is to ask yourself a couple of questions:

How relevant is their message to what I do on a day-in-and-day-out basis; and to what extent did it change the way I behave, communicate or interact with the people around me?

In terms of relevancy to what you do, I can confidently say that if you are in sales, especially the healthcare sales field, *What's Your Sales Story?* is not only relevant to you, but it will profoundly change the way that you sell to your customer.

Those of us who in the healthcare industry are privileged to interact with educated individuals who, first and foremost, hold patient care as the single most important aspect of their work. Never should we take for granted the time and the access that healthcare professionals provide us. To that point, *What's Your Sales Story?* transcends obvious sales principles and helps ensure that time with customers is beneficial and productive for everyone involved. The author's style and approach are unique. Ja Marr Brown engages the reader on a number of different levels. He shares his story as a sales professional in the healthcare industry and employs written exercises at the end of each chapter that will assist readers to understand and develop their own stories.

Brown's story is no fairytale–it is brutally honest, candid, amusing and insightful. *What's Your Sales Story?* is the true account of a young, rookie pharmaceutical sales representative whose ego trips him up more times than a vaudeville comedian on a banana skin! As the story unfolds, so does the realization that his style and approach was, in a word, misguided. Slowly, the light goes on, and Brown sees why he needs to make meaningful changes and then shows the reader how to do it by applying the Kaizen principles. In the end, he not only becomes the company's #1 sales rep and a mentor to many throughout the organization, but he also grows into better person.

When you cut right through the myriad of sales techniques and principles, what you end up with is that people buy from those they trust and respect. Trust and respect is as much about what you sell as to who you are. The cost of entry is products that make a difference; that's a given. But the ability to create enduring relationships with the customers can only be cultivated by the sales rep. There is no more effective way to communicate who you are than to know and share your own story. And there is no better way to establish trust and rapport with your customer than to listen and know their story as they share it with you.

What's Your Sales Story? is a book that should be read by individuals in the healthcare selling field. Furthermore, the observations and the exercises are applicable and relevant to any industry. No matter if you just started your sales career or you're a seasoned veteran, this book is written and designed for you.

As the North American president of a pharmaceutical company, I encourage my management peers to read and learn from this book. The ability for management to connect and motivate their sales force *(if you are able to tell your own story)* is every bit as important as the sales force being successful in front of their audience, the customer.

Julian Gangolli
President North America
Allergan Inc.

DEDICATION

This book is dedicated to the "Why" in my life, my daughter, Alexis Brown.

ACKNOWLEDGEMENTS

It is 1:43 AM. As usual, I am reflecting on my life and writing out my thoughts: God has truly blessed me, and I give thanks for the experiences I have had, and the people who have inspired and influenced me throughout my journey. At 34, I have no regrets and have come to understand my ultimate purpose. That understanding could not have come if I had not *listened and applied* the life lessons that countless people have bestowed upon me. As I have always said, I never forget those individuals who have touched my life. This book represents my gratitude to all of those individuals. In addition, it is as a rare opportunity to put their stories and lessons in a form that will live on just as their teachings will continue to shape my life. I can think of no better way to say thank you.

As we pursue our dreams, sacrifices are inevitable, but there are times when they seem insurmountable. I could not have written *What's Your Sales Story?* without the love and support of my family. First and foremost, I want to thank my parents, Bettye and Roosevelt Brown, for teaching me that the role of a parent is to ensure that their children's lives are better than their own. They also instilled in me an undying hunger and passion for knowledge and wisdom. To my brothers: Roosevelt, Jr., Malcolm and Ja Bari, for igniting my competitive spirit; they never let me settle for being less than I was capable of. To my wife, Amanda, the most honest and real person I ever have met. Thank you for challenging and encouraging me to pursue my dreams. And finally, to my daughter, Alexis: Being your father is the greatest gift God has ever given me!

I also would like to thank those individuals who helped me directly or indirectly with *What's Your Sales Story?* Julian Gangoli; Michael Hill; Hector Lafarga, Jr (Inroads); Alex Lopez; Glen March, M.D.; Derek and Lacy Matthews; James Peace, M.D.; Rob Seguin.; Laura Spaulding; Jim Trunick; and Jane Wolf. And finally, to my good friend and mentor, Sarah Taylor: Being involved with your book inspired me to write mine!

Special thanks to those individuals who helped me with the physical creation of *What's Your Sales Story?* Pete Nelson at Everywhere Marketing; your friendship, support and guidance are key reasons why this book exists. Maggi Mormomisato, my editor; thank you for making *What's Your Sales Story?* your own.

Lastly, I want to thank you, the reader, for opening yourself up to a new way of learning how to achieve sales success. It is my hope that along the way, the lessons you took from *What's Your Sales Story?* will be the start of or the continuation of success in both your professional and personal life.

Please share your thoughts with me at
www.Whatsyoursalesstory.com.

TABLE OF CONTENTS

Introduction

"Storytelling reveals meaning."
~ Hannah Arendt ~

What's Your Sales Story? is written for anyone who sells for a living.

This is not your typical 10-habits type of book on sales. Unlike other books on sales that you have read, you won't find any clichéd sales strategies, outdated theories or generic examples. What you are about to read is 100% reality. The situations and stories are true, with only the names of the people involved in the stories omitted or changed.

Let's face it, while it's true there are some fundamental aspects of successful selling that haven't changed, the world we sell in certainly has. Therefore, to be ahead of the curve, it's critical that salespeople learn techniques and skills with real-world applications. This is critical in order to stay relevant and ahead of your competition.

When it comes to perennial success in sales, there is no better educator than real-life stories of others who have traveled the path you want to go down. With that in mind, what you will discover is a new form of sales education I refer to as *Reality-Based Sales.*

Teaching You Through You

Success in life and sales is not about a specific number of habits or tips. It's about stories. Stories are formed by experiences, and this book will help you understand how your experiences have shaped you as a person and sales professional. This will occur as you learn from my sales experiences, and complete the exercises and action steps at the end of each chapter.

Success in life and sales is not about a specific number of habits or tips. It's about stories.

You will learn as much or more about yourself as you do about me. Together, we will identify your past, write your history and define your future. But it won't be just any future: it will be the one you always have dreamed of living.

Although I reference my experience in the medical device and pharmaceutical industries, the lessons from my story, along with the exercises at the end of each chapter, are applicable and relevant to any sales industry. Whether you are a novice salesperson or a seasoned veteran, this book is written and designed for you.

In teaching you how to use your story for achieving consistent sales success, I will share my story, in all of its painful and triumphant detail, with you, which includes the very same lessons that transformed me from a relatively obscure, self-absorbed, young summer intern to the top sales professional for one of the most successful and respected pharmaceutical companies in the world.

A Promise & the Why

A pivotal reason for my success can be traced to a five-minute encounter with a little-old-lady in a doctor's office. I promised her that I would dedicate my career to helping and teaching other professionals just as she had helped me by sharing her story. Writing this book is just one of the ways that I have kept my promise. You will learn more about this incredible woman as you read further in the book.

While the encounter with that woman and her story forever changed how I looked at selling, the Why behind writing this book came from my daughter, Alexis. She is my biggest inspiration and the driving force behind everything I do at this stage of my life. Having a book for my daughter that documents my journey through a pivotal period of my life is a significant part of why this book exists.

What This Book Covers

The journey you are about to take within these pages will allow you to get to know yourself, again. You will gain life-changing insight into some of the most vital elements of selling, just not in the way you would have been accustomed to or may have expected.

You will learn who and what you are all about as well as where you come from, and where you are going in your career. You will uncover your hidden truths, quiet fears and overlooked limitations. You will come face to face with your past and learn how to harness its answers in order to map out the future as you envision it. You will unlock the code to what is holding you back from achieving consistent and perennial success in sales and in life.

Will you learn how to improve your current sales efforts? Yes. But this book isn't about closing or handling objections. This book completely redefines what it takes to master a well-crafted and rehearsed sales presentation. You will learn how to win in any sales situation and transform yourself into a perennial sales performer.

By learning the lessons from my own story, coupled with the exercises in the book, you will learn the secrets behind listening to and applying your customers' stories to the sales process. You will begin to learn how to spot areas in your career where your ego has gotten in the way of your sales success. Most importantly, you will learn how to manage your ego by understanding the stories you tell yourself and others.

The Ego's Story

It's been said that to succeed in sales you must possess a healthy sized ego. But what exactly does that mean? For most, it means that the bigger the ego, the easier it is to bounce back from rejection. The ego, though, is much more than just how highly you think of yourself or the amount of confidence you exude. When it comes to succeeding in sales, it's not the size of your ego that matters but how you manage it.

According to some psychologists, the ego is defined as an illusionary sense of "self." The ego's main goal is to protect itself and maintain an illusion instead of reality. When it comes to one's true purpose in life, psychologists consider this thought process as the reason behind why money, power, greed and self-indulgence is placed above goodwill, spiritual and personal growth.

From the stories we tell ourselves to the stories others tell us, our ego is behind how we interpret them. Whether the stories are helping or hurting us, they tend to play repeatedly in our heads. The recurring themes produce a pattern of behavior. For salespeople, when the ego is involved, the pattern of behavior that results is both common and predictable.

Depending on the stories your ego has fed you about success, you may embrace it or you may be fearful of it. For many salespeople, when they experience success, they get so wrapped up in their accomplishments that they forget how they achieved it and lose sight of why they are selling. The end result is usually a crash landing into reality as they soon find themselves struggling, unable to repeat their earlier successes.

> *When it comes to succeeding in sales, it's not the size of your ego that matters but how you manage it.*

When things are not going well, salespeople's egos are known to weave elaborate stories that deflect responsibility from themselves. They convince themselves and others that their setbacks and failures are out of their control. The following are a few examples:

- *There are no more opportunities in my territory;*
- *The compensation plan is unfair;*
- *My customers don't like me;*

• *Sales are always low during this quarter; or*
• *The products I have to sell don't do everything they're supposed to.*

Do any of those sound familiar? If they do, it's because you've either used one or more of them yourself, or you've heard them from other sales professionals. The good thing is that these debilitating stories can be stopped. In order to move your ego out of the way of your sales success, you will want to start by rediscovering the primary reason *Why* you sell.

Perennial Sales Performers

I am often asked what separates the average salesperson from the perennial sales performer. My answer is always the same. Perennial sales performers know, understand and fully utilize their stories to engage, communicate and connect with their customers. Average salespeople do not.

This answer isn't always easily understood at first and for good reason. Rarely do you hear a salesperson's story cited in books or training programs as critically important to success in sales. The surprised and sometimes skeptical responses quickly go away, though, once it's understood just how often we all use stories in our personal and professional lives to communicate.

This book will help you identify your personal story and guide you through the process of writing it. Writing your story is not about how grammatically correct you are or the eloquent words you choose. It is about understanding the *Why* behind your efforts.

Everything you think about and act on each day pulls you closer to your desired outcomes or pushes you further away from them. The direction by which you choose to go is navigated by your

> *Writing your story is not about how grammatically correct you are or the eloquent words you choose. It is about understanding the Why behind your efforts.*

Why, which is the underlying motivation for what you do.

Why you sell isn't about making money. Making money is a by product of *Why* you sell. For example, if you're a sales veteran nearing retirement, money will be represented by a completely different *Why* than if you're just starting out in your career.

To truly become a great salesperson, you must have a clearly defined *Why* that is bigger than simply making the sale and earning a commission. Remember, anyone can sell, but not everyone becomes a perennial sales performer.

What's In a Story?

Stories are not just an integral part of sales success; they are the very fabric that runs through all human interactions, framing our perspective of the world we live in.

Stories uplift our spirit and stir our emotions. They awaken our soul and breathe hope into despair. Stories shape and define entire cultures. They teach and provide perspective. They build companies and grow careers. And nothing ever gets sold without a story being told.

Throughout history, stories have been used to teach, entertain, honor spiritual beliefs, settle disputes, express love, and they have been used to sell. Take, for example, the story of David and Goliath or the Boy Who Cried Wolf. They contain universal themes and messages that can be applied to any culture or situation. As a result, those two stories have been used around the world to inspire and guide people socially and morally.

According to the Kalahari Bushmen, recognized as the oldest living culture on earth, a person's story is viewed as his most treasured resource. From our birth to our passing, stories serve as the backbone of our existence, both personally and professionally.

Stories Unlock the Customer Code

Stories provide customers with a frame of reference for making decisions. Stories also shape the customers' perspectives of the products and services they seek as well as the brands and companies from which they buy. Because of that, companies spend millions of dollars training their salespeople on the stories behind their products and services, so they can convey them to customers. Billions of dollars are spent on telling those stories to customers through marketing and branding campaigns.

What good, however, is the story of your product or even the stories of your customers, if your salespeople don't know their own stories?

For far too long, I've seen well intentioned sales professionals, their confidence masked by insecurities they refuse to acknowledge, attempt to get by with antiquated sales tactics, strategies and yes, stories, that simply don't work. This is especially true today.

Customers are savvier as to when, why and from whom they make purchases. Choices for where to buy and who to buy from are more abundant. Loyalty has become the exception rather than the rule. Customers simply do not tolerate average salespeople to the degree they used to.

Think about the customers you call on: If they have had bad experiences with salespeople, making a sale will be an uphill battle unless you can first change their perception of who they think you are.

Whether the stories customers have told themselves about salespeople are distorted or 100% accurate, if they believe salespeople are unethical, rude and only out to make a sale is how you will be viewed. To change their perspective, you will have to help them rewrite new versions of their stories.

The first step to changing their perspective is to listen and learn your customers' stories, one by one, and then apply what you learn to the sales process. You will find that this creates a smoother sale, and you no longer will have to force the close. Instead, you will become the facilitator as your customers, close themselves. Before you can learn their stories, though, you must first understand your own.

Your Story Matters

Your story matters because your experiences matter. How you interpret and leverage your experiences ultimately will determine the level of success you enjoy in life and your career.

Selling isn't just about you or your company's solution. A majority of salespeople forget that on a daily basis. Instead, they focus on getting the sale rather than getting to know the customer. When you discover how to leverage your experiences during a sales call in a way that gets your customers to comfortably reveal information about themselves, you eliminate your need to be the star of the sale. Once the spotlight is on your customers, they are more prone to share crucial pieces of information that moves the sales process along.

Before you can learn your customers' stories, you must first understand your own.

To hear their stories and then apply those stories to the sales process takes more than simple listening skills, however. The customers will give you clues throughout the sales call, and it will be imperative that you are aware of them. The following are some examples of clues:

- Career and personal life;
- What moves them as individuals;
- What they think about previous sales reps; and/or
- Why they like or dislike your competitor's products.

Their stories shape and mold their view of the world, including how they view you, your company and your solution.

If you can learn the meaning behind your customer's stories, you will have unlocked an important code into how they make decisions to buy. Doing so makes the sale much easier for you and your customers.

Getting the Most Out of the Book

To eliminate waste and maximize your time reading and applying what is in the book, I carefully outlined this book in three ways.

One, you'll be able to immerse yourself into my story, learning some valuable lessons on how to face and handle the failures and successes in sales.

Two, each chapter is set up to build on the previous chapter, and there are spaces throughout the chapters to write your own personal story.

Three, if you need more space in order to do justice to your story, there is a companion workbook, which is in Word format, available at www.WhatsYourSalesStory.com/workbookcompanion. You will be able to easily download it for use as a roadmap to uncovering your personal story.

Let's Start the Journey

When some people buy books, they tend to flip through the pages as if they're browsing a restaurant menu. If you choose to do that with *What's Your Sales Story?* or you opt to hide behind the story you've been telling yourself for years, then your "real" story may never surface, and you could be denied the life you were meant to live.

The key to perennial sales success cannot be discovered through basking in your accomplishments or dwelling on your failures. It's found in continuing to follow and learn from your "Life's Story," which has made you who you are.

So, grab a pen. Open your mind and get mentally comfortable. Now, let's begin your journey. Your story awaits you.

CHAPTER 1
What's In a Name?

"I am part of all that I have met."

~ Tennyson ~

It's 6:30 on a Saturday morning. For most, this is a time to sleep in, an opportunity to recharge one's self from the stress, worries and anxieties of the previous week. For me, it's reflection time. There is something invigorating about the quiet stillness on an early Saturday morning that jumpstarts my creative juices.

Normally I head to the local coffee shop with a book or my personal journal in hand. That particular morning, however, I found myself in the living room of our new home rummaging through the unpacked boxes. I had decided that if I were to spend half of my early-morning hours reflecting, it would be best to do so by surprising my wife and begin organizing the "junk" left over from our recent move.

I started with the living room cabinets, where a collection of old VHS tapes had been haphazardly thrown in. As I began taking each of them out, two titles caught my eye: *"Ja Marr & Amanda's Wedding"* and *"Lexi's 1st Birthday."*

Memories washed over me, and I was immediately transported to those seminal moments in my life. I closed my eyes and remembered all of the failed pickup lines I initially used to get my wife, Amanda, to go out with me. When I asked if she would like to go out for ice cream, I'll never forget the smile on her face or her answer, "Now there's a line I haven't heard before. Yes, I'll go out for ice cream with you."

The scene shifted in my mind; then I was watching our beautiful daughter as she playfully opened gifts on her first birthday, more amused by the wrapping paper than by the gifts themselves.

I opened my eyes and couldn't help but smile. I decided

to place those videos off to the side, knowing they would be something my family and I would watch again. I kept going through the videos, putting most of them into a box. And then one jumped out at me and stopped me in my tracks. Unlike the contents of the other two videos, this title sent a mixture of emotions through me that I had not felt in more than 10 years. An odd sensation of anxiousness yet curious wonderment drove me to the family room. I placed the video, whose title read, *"Allergan Awards 1998/1999,"* into the VCR. I sat back on the sofa waiting for the images to emerge.

> *He was seen as the best- of-the best in a company whose sales force was rated as # 1 in the industry. The truth is he wasn't.*

The president of Allergan was on stage speaking before the entire company's sales force and most of its top executives.

"This next person is truly an inspiration and an incredible success story. He began his career in 1993 as a summer intern at Allergan. Upon graduation, he joined as a full-time sales rep in Los Angeles. Last year, he was ranked # 91 in the country. Within 12 months, he shot all the way up to #1. He also was recently promoted to Senior Territory Manager. Not only is he one of the youngest sales reps in the history of Allergan to win this next award, but he has distinguished himself as simply the best-of-the-best. Ladies and gentleman, please join me in welcoming to the stage our 1998 Salesperson of the Year…"

You could barely hear the name as the applause from the crowd drowned out the last part of the introduction. I sat there intently watching as a young 24-year-old man confidently strode up to the podium and shook hands with the president of Allergan.

As the crowd gave a standing ovation, I felt my emotions change from one of intrigue and intense curiosity to disbelief. I actually started to laugh at what I had just heard and was now reliving. It had been nearly 10 years since I had attended this annual event and was able to view it from a unique vantage point. What I found funny was the fact that the young man receiving the Salesperson of the Year award had been seen as the best-of-the best in a company whose sales force was rated as # 1 in the industry. The truth is, he wasn't. And I couldn't help but recognize the harsh irony of it all.

I know, because that 24-year-old young man was me.

In the Blink of an Eye

I paused the video. In the blink of an eye, I had seen my life, at least the life that was on that video tape, flash before me. Leaning back into the sofa, I reflected on what had been my ultimate goal as a sales professional: win the coveted Salesperson of the Year Award. I had first dreamt of winning and delivering an acceptance speech back in 1993 when I initially walked into the company as a 19-year-old summer intern. Allergan had decided to become a sponsoring company of the INROADS internship program and had selected me as their first intern.

I immediately made a point of familiarizing myself with some of the past salespeople of the year. They were the ones that everyone talked about and revered at Allergan. From the respect they commanded to the six-figure salaries they earned, they were the rock stars at the company. I was in awe of them. In my mind, there was absolutely no doubt that I would ascend the same steps and join their ranks on that stage in Hawaii. It didn't matter to me how hard the journey would be, because I was confident enough in my abilities to know that I would get there.

Those mental images from the past were so vivid that I literally relived every emotion from that time in my life right up to the point when I was back sitting there on my sofa. Certain images that flooded my mind had made me laugh, others reminded me of the pain I went through and actually brought tears to my eyes. Some left me bewildered, with questions still unanswered while others seemed to shake me to my core, humbling me all over again.

And now here I was about to relive my Salesperson-of-the-Year acceptance speech. But first, let me take a moment and address what you might already be thinking. If I was not the best-of-the-best, how was I was able to go from virtually last place in sales ranking, nearly get fired and then end up as the top sales rep in one of the most competitive industries in the world? Believe me, I often wondered the same thing. And what made it even more difficult to grasp was that I had accomplished this after only two-and-one-half years from officially joining the company.

Let's clear up a couple of things right away. I was not what you would classify as a natural-born salesperson or a seasoned sales professional. Sure, I had more than two years of experience in the field and had interned at Allergan for two summers. Even so, Allergan represented a major step up in professional selling that few industries can prepare you for, and, despite my internship, I had virtually zero sales experience – in any industry! As a matter of fact, as an intern, my ability to understand and communicate the clinical sales messages was so bad that Allergan had me selling shoes during role-plays instead of the company's own products.

I was confident in my abilities but also realized I needed to work twice as hard as anyone else. From countless hours perfecting my sales presentation to reading every clinical study that was available, there wasn't much I didn't memorize or practice. Yet, for nearly two-and-one-half years, my position barely budged from the bottom of the sales rankings. It did not matter how hard I worked or how confident I remained, I could not move up the rankings.

So the question remained, "How did I do it?" I was wondering the very same thing. After a few more moments of reliving my story in my mind, I mustered up enough courage and pressed play, again, on the VCR.

What's In a Name?

Watching the video, the answer began to surface. I listened intently to the acceptance speech I delivered in Hawaii. Not once did I refer to my sales skills, ability to close or increased market share. There was no mention of major accounts that I had secured or how I was able to leverage my relationships. As a matter of fact, I refrained from using business terms or sales jargon altogether as a means to my success. Listening, I was reminded that I originally had intended to cover those things. In the end, I had thrown that speech away. Instead, I referred only to a single index card that contained the most important names in my sales career.

They represented the lessons, the triumphs and setbacks as well as my growth, not just as a pharmaceutical sales professional, but as a man.

Each name on that index card represented a person who had played a pivotal role in the defining moments of my sales story and journey from the time I was an intern to becoming Salesperson of the Year. They represented the lessons, triumphs and setbacks as well as my growth, not just as a pharmaceutical sales professional, but as a man. They were the reason I stood before more than 400 people, accepting the most prestigious award given to sales professionals.

As I read off the names from the index card on the video, my recollection of each person ran vividly through my mind. Their faces, their words and the encounters we had had through the years. Some of them, I met only once. Others, I had continuous interactions with, even to this day. All played a critical role in preparing me for the transition I made from where I had been to where I am, today: Salesperson of the Year; Seven major promotions in 10 years; Handled the marketing for one of Allergan's biggest and most ambitious product launches; Area manager of the Year; And, finally, at age 32, one of the youngest

Regional Sales Directors at Allergan—directly responsible for nine sales managers, 80 territory managers and more than $250 million in sales.

I did not accomplish any of those things alone.

Those names were the reason why I did not give up and quit when I was virtually in last place. Those names were responsible for how I was able to accomplish the impossible and take a sales territory that had never done better than the bottom 30% in the country and move it to first place. Those names represented the people who taught me the mindset, leadership, preparation and sales skills necessary to rise to the top and stay there.

None of them are best-selling authors. They are not sales or leadership gurus. And, unless you're related to them or friends of theirs, I doubt you've ever heard of them.

If I did not do it alone, what, then, can I take credit for— listening to and applying what they taught me to the sales process. My story, however, is not as simple as receiving good advice and applying it. Boy, do I wish it were! As you will soon discover, my story, like so many other's, is anything but predictable.

I want you to stop reading this book for a moment.

Your journey toward discovering your story begins right now.

The following three exercises mark the beginning of the steps that will take you through the process of developing your own story. Each exercise is specifically tied to the theme of the chapter that precedes it.

Reminder → Be sure to visit www.WhatsYourSalesStory.com/ workbookcompanion to download the companion workbook. While at our site don't forget to share your sales story and check out the latest tips and techniques designed to help you become a perennial sales performer.

STEP 1: Who Are You?

The first step in writing your story is to determine just how much you really know yourself. On the lines provided below, describe yourself as a person.

This is not always as easy as it may seem, so be sure to give yourself both time and permission to discover the answer.

Tip ➜ After you've written out your description, put it to the test by asking someone close to you to describe how they perceive you. Are there any inconsistencies?

Be sure to also do this with customers. In fact, I would highly recommend you do this with at least two or three of your customers.

Describe Yourself:

_____

_____

_____

_____

_____

_____

_____

STEP 2: Your Index Card

Best-selling author Les Brown once said that you ask for help not because you're weak, but because you want to remain strong. Whether you directly asked for help or not, there are people you've come across in your life and career who either guided or influenced you enough that they left an indelible mark, shaping you into the person you are today.

What Names Are On Your Index Card?
The second step in writing your story is discovering the names of five (5) people who have played a pivotal role in your sales career. When you have those names, place them on your index card.

At first this may seem like a simple exercise. It isn't. For example, you might be inclined to write your parents' names, a close relative or maybe a dear friend who always has stood by your side. None of those names would be wrong, so if that is the case, by all means list them. *But the names I'm talking about are those you've encountered along the way in your career.*

Tip → As you consider what names to write down, think about the following:

A satisfied or even disgruntled customer that changed your perspective of your career; A manager who believed in you more than you believed in yourself; A manager who didn't believe in you yet taught you more about who you are than you would have expected; A colleague who supported you.

As you think of the names, consider what each person has meant to you. To help, you may want to write down what it was that they did or said that made such an impact on you. Think about how you met them and where you were in life when you encountered them.

STEP 2: Your Index Card (continued)

Identify and list the five names below:

1. _____

2. _____

3. _____

4. _____

5. _____

STEP 3: What is Your *Why*?

Now, let's shift our focus to your motivation for unlocking the story within you. Remember, your story is bigger than you and goes beyond just you.

In the book's Introduction you read about my primary inspirations for telling my story, such as my daughter. In the following chapters you will learn how these inspirations touched everyone I came in contact with.

Just as it was for me, your story will touch the lives of others. But who is it that your story will touch and how? Some you will have names for while others you may have no idea. For now, I want you to stop reading this chapter and uncover the following:

Who or what will serve as the inspiration for you to write your story? In other words, who or what is your *Why*?

_____

_____

_____

_____

Now that you have a clearer sense of why you're writing your story, it's time to determine **who your story matters to and why**? I've provided some helpful anchors to get you going.

To You:

_____

_____

_____

_____

STEP 3: What is Your *Why*? (continued)

To Your Family & Friends:

_____

_____

_____

_____

To Your Customers:

_____

_____

_____

_____

_____

Reminder → Be sure to visit www.WhatsYourSalesStory.com/workbookcompanion to download the companion workbook. While at our site don't forget to share your sales story and check out the latest tips and techniques designed to help you become a perennial sales performer.

CHAPTER 2
How Your Ego Gets In The Way of Success

"I followed my EGO and ended up alone."
~Ja Marr Brown ~

It was fall 1994; I was a senior in college and unlike many of my friends, I knew exactly what I was going to do after graduation.

At this point, I had already gone through five interviews for full-time positions at major companies post graduation. At the conclusion of each interview process, I was offered a job. A couple of the companies actually got into bidding wars over me.

After a lot of thought and discussion with my parents and those close to me, I made the decision that would forever change the course of my life. I would to go to work for Allergan Pharmaceuticals.

In the end, it wasn't really that difficult of a decision. I had, after all, interned at Allergan for the past two summers as part of the INROADS Internship Program.

To learn more about INROADS, visit www.inroads.org

I was young, had never faced any real setbacks or disappointments in my life up to that point and was feeling pretty good. Scratch that. I felt invincible.

Do You Know Who I Am?

My new boss sat across from me and officially welcomed me, "We're all really excited to have you on board at Allergan full time, Ja Marr. You're going to initially work in the Los Angeles (LA) territory. It's in the bottom of the country in terms of sales rankings. In fact, it's never finished higher than the bottom 30%. It's just a bad territory, so the expectations for you will be minimal."

I remember thinking, "minimal expectations? Who does this guy think he's talking to?"

He went on to say, "I want you to know that the LA territory is being viewed as a developmental assignment and not a permanent place for you. It's just for you to get acclimated to the industry and learn the job. You will be assigned there for 18 months and then, as soon as an opening in a better territory is available we'll move you there. That's when you'll start making some serious money."

It was May 1995, and I was barely two weeks removed from graduation. Remember when I said I was feeling invincible while I was in college? Well, that paled in comparison to the level of confidence I felt sitting across from my new boss.

"First off, let me just say I am really excited to be a part of Allergan, too," I said. "And I hear what you are saying about the LA territory, but I will be the #1 salesperson at Allergan. I am going to make LA the #1 territory in the country."

I could not believe t his was my boss. Wasn't he supposed to support me? Wasn't he supposed to encourage me?

He must have thought that I was joking, because he immediately started to laugh and replied, "Number 1 in LA? I don't think so. It just isn't gonna happen."

Before I realized what I was saying, I fired back, "Yes, it will."

He just shook his head and reminded me that it would never happen.

I thought I would humor him and asked, "Why don't you think I can be Salesperson of the Year?"

"It's simple,' he said, as if I should have known the answer myself. "First of all, you don't know the business well enough to even say that. Secondly, you're a bit too eager. In order to be successful in sales, you have to be patient and really take the time to learn the business inside and out. You are overly focused on the end result and not the process required to achieve those results."

My grip on the chair tightened, and I literally was gritting my teeth. I could not believe this was my boss. Wasn't he supposed to support me? Wasn't he supposed to encourage me?

He must have known that I wasn't getting It, because he continued to hammer home his point. "Like I told you, Ja Marr, the LA territory has never done well. It always has and always will be at the bottom of the rankings. That's how it has been and that's how it will always be. There's absolutely nothing you or I can do about it."

He could see that this didn't sit well with me. "Ja Marr, you have a tremendous amount of potential. This is nothing more than an 18-month developmental assignment. Don't take the fact that this territory is bad as a knock against your potential. After this period is over, you will realize your full potential in another territory."

His words of encouragement didn't help. He stood up and extended his hand, which I reluctantly shook. As I did, I looked him straight in the eyes and confidently declared, "I will be #1. And I will do it this year."

I walked out of the office determined to back up my claim. As I strode past the offices of the senior executives of the company, I couldn't help but think to myself, "No matter what it takes, I am going to show everyone in this company what I am capable of. They hire me and then doubt my abilities? I'm going to be #1 and do it in a territory nobody believes in."

Of course, the fact that it was already May, and I had only seven months in the year to transform a territory ranked 138 out of 140 to #1 didn't faze me one bit. In my mind, there was just no way I could fail.

STEP 4: The State of Your Ego

Take the next several moments and describe the state of mind your ego placed you in when you first started your career.

Were you scared? Nervous? Anxious? Fearless? Arrogant? Was it innocence or ignorance that led your decisions and actions at that time in your life? Or for those of you who may be getting ready to enter into sales for the first time, what emotions are you currently experiencing?

To help guide you through this step in developing your story, use the following question to base your answer:

What was the state of your ego when you started your career?

_____

_____

_____

_____

A Thirst for Knowledge

There were seven months to go in the year. I was a rookie rep in one of the toughest industries to sell in, assigned to one of the worst territories in the country. And outside of what I learned as an intern, I had zero sales experience.

Despite the obstacles I faced or the odds against me, I confidently set out in May 1995, to prove to Allergan and to myself that I would become the #1 salesperson in the company.

My ego was enormous at the time. Even so, I understood

that no matter how confident I was in my abilities, I still needed to work harder than anyone else. I may have been naïve but not so much so that I thought everything just would be handed to me.

I attended three weeks of new-hire training and was awarded top honors for all new hires. Following the end of the class, I was relentless in my pursuit of knowledge. I continued to study everything Allergan had produced with respect to clinical studies and product guides. I reread the manual from class nearly every day and devoured every book on sales I could find. I remember talking with some of the other new hires who were in my training class, and they were shocked by the sheer amount of material I was reading. Sure, I was competitive and certainly driven to succeed in my new career, but this insatiable appetite for knowledge had more to do with my father than it did for simply succeeding as a sales professional.

For as long as I can remember, my father instilled a thirst a knowledge in my brothers and me, which, in turn, was fueled by a passion for reading. Many family nights consisted of my father asking us questions on a variety of subjects from ancient Roman philosophy to geography and the definition of the most uncommon words. He would have us research our answers by utilizing any one of the hundreds of books he had collected over the years. My brothers and I were in awe of his knowledge and were always competing against each other to come up with the right answers.

Eventually, my father took his passion for knowledge and books, and formed a program called, Reading Literacy Learning. Dedicated to promoting learning and literacy among children in the lower socioeconomic areas in San Diego, the program has been recognized for giving out more than 1 million brand new books to children at his annual Children's Book Party (www.childrensbookparty.org). This event always served as an inspiration and reminder to me of just how important knowledge and books were to life.

Now, many years later, I was applying what my father taught me about the importance of knowledge. I started with Dale Carnegie's book, *How to Win Friends and Influence People*, which my father had given me when I was 12 years old. This time, instead of competing against my brothers to find the answers, I was competing against an entire sales force, all of whom had their eyes on the #1 spot in the rankings.

How the Ego Sets You Up

Knowledge, in and of itself isn't useful. What matters is to use it to achieve a desired outcome. With that in mind, each day, I reviewed and mastered Allergan's sales process and developed a solid sales presentation. I stood in front of the mirror many times, imagining the doctors I would be calling on, and I practiced my sales presentation, carefully dissecting every nuance in my speech and expressions. It wasn't long before I felt I could go toe-to-toe with any physician on any subject relating to our products – and win.

I truly felt that I had stacked the odds in my favor, and I was going to be Salesperson of the Year.

In the field, I didn't leave anything to chance. Implementing the detailed and focused territory-management-system I had designed, I planned my calls meticulously, noting the best times to see each physician. My system was based on zip codes, office hours and surgery schedules. I was not about to waste my time visiting a doctor's office, unannounced, in the hopes that the physician was available. There was no value for me or the doctor by stopping in and waiting for 20 minutes or longer just to give a sound bite and leave some samples. I wanted real interaction and dialogue. More than that, I felt I deserved, and often times demanded, more face time with my customers.

Two months into my new position, I was more confident than ever that my efforts would bring me to my ultimate goal. It didn't matter that I was brand new to this job and industry. It didn't matter that my sales experience paled in comparison to other more seasoned sales veterans. I truly felt that I had stacked the odds in my favor, and I was going to be Salesperson of the Year.

In February 1996, the 1995 year-to-date sales rankings came out. I was ranked 135 out of 140. In seven months, despite all of my efforts and outworking a majority of the other reps, I only had moved up three spots.

Doubling My Efforts

The fact that I had only moved up three spots did not deter me. The way I rationalized it was that I needed a little more time. If I could not become #1 in seven months, then no one could. I was ok with that.

My outlook on 1996 was even more intense and focused, because I decided that to reach the top, I would need to double my efforts.

For the next 12 months, I led my entire district in calls-per-day and details-per-call. This wasn't about the number of phone calls or computer clicks but actual sales calls. I was using the same system I previously had developed, but I was scheduling calls right at the time the physician's office opened or, in many cases, when it was closing. Whether I was the first or last person that the doctor saw, I was determined that, one way or another, we would be meeting. While I didn't realize it at the time, my actions took on the tone that was more akin to the proverbial bull in a china shop than that of a seasoned, sales professional!

For the first few months of the year, I wasn't moving up the rankings at all. As the months passed, I continued to be on the bottom. I thought that it was because I was not working hard enough or not using enough resources. My plan for rectifying that was to lead the team in resource utilization. That meant tapping into the resources that Allergan had to help the doctors I called on. As a result, I put on more dinner programs and consultants meetings than any other rep in my area. If there was a resource to leverage, I leveraged it to the hilt.

I continued studying after work hours. At one point, I knew the products and clinical studies so well that I became the district point person for technical questions and information. Despite what the monthly rankings showed, I had no doubt that I was on the verge of making the greatest turnaround in the history of the company. This prevailing thought kept me motivated to push myself and work harder than anybody else in my district.

STEP 5: Giving It Your All

At this point in my story, I absolutely was convinced that the key to being the best salesperson was work ethic. Want to reach your goals? Work hard. Not getting the results you want? Work harder. If someone tells you that you can't achieve something? Then work even harder than before.

During your career, especially at the beginning stages, have you ever found yourself answering those questions the same way as I did? Have you ever had a goal in your career or your personal life where you felt you were giving everything you had – the blood, sweat and tears – yet, the results you desired weren't coming fast enough?

In the space provided below, I want you to write about a specific incident in your career. Or for those of you that are new to sales, consider a time in your life where you gave it your all, but it just was not good enough.

Tip ➜ Don't jump ahead and write about the outcome and how you may have achieved or didn't achieve your goals. *For now, just focus on describing the actual effort you were putting forth and the amount of energy you were exerting.* We will address the results of those actions later in the book.

_____

_____

_____

The Moment of Truth

I woke up early February 28, 1997, knowing today was the day. The year-to-date rankings were scheduled to be released. There always was a two-month delay in the actual data. Since it was very possible for reps to significantly rise in the rankings, I felt I had done enough to make that leap and eagerly anticipated the results.

I can still remember the sound of my cell phone ringing and my anticipation of the news my boss was about to give me.

"Ja Marr, I want to let you know how proud of you I am for working as hard as you did this past year. You've come a long way, and you've set yourself up for a lot of success this year."

"Success this year?" I thought to myself. "Isn't he going to tell me that I was successful last year? When's he going to let me know that I won Salesperson of the Year, instead of going on about how I was setting an example for the new reps as well as some of the veterans on the team." I thought that he was toying with me, so I just blurted, "How did I finish last year?"

He said, "Ja Marr, this year will be your year; let's just put last year behind us."

Confused, I replied, "I don't understand. What do you mean put last year behind us? I finished at the top didn't I?"

There was a deafening silence on the other line. It seemed like minutes, but only a few seconds had passed when my boss said, "Ja Marr, you finished 130 out of 140."

I remember saying that there must be a mistake, and there's no way, with the efforts I put in, especially during October through December, that my numbers didn't go up.

I reminded him that I had led the district in every productivity measure (sales calls per day, details per call, utilization of resources, etc.), and no one knew the product information better than I did. I asked him to call the data people and have them double check my results. He agreed to do that and said he'd get back with me to verify everything.

I felt some relief when we hung up because I just knew there had been a mistake in the data. Within 45 minutes, everything was confirmed.

My cell phone rang, and it was my boss on the other end. "Ja Marr, there was no mistake, you finished 130 out of 140," he said.

At some point, he added some encouraging words, none of which I heard. My mind was consumed with the idea that for the first time in my life, I had failed. Until now, I had never failed at anything. What added insult to injury was that I couldn't have tried any harder. I gave my absolute best and even that was not good enough to get out of the bottom ranking. I was devastated.

Denny's

After my manager delivered that sobering news, I found it difficult to muster up enough motivation to make sales calls that day. But I decided that there was nothing I could do to improve my ranking by staying home. I stopped at Denny's before my first sales call. After that gut-wrenching call, I needed something in my stomach. It was just after 9 a.m., when I slid into a corner booth. Six hours later, I was still there.

I replayed the past year in my mind, over and over. I was searching for some kind of answer as to why I didn't win Salesperson of the Year, let alone barely move in the rankings. I recalled every physician I had spoken to, every dinner program I had put on and the countless hours spent studying clinical trials and product information sheets. I thought about all the sacrifices I had made. Now it seemed like such a waste.

I felt so ashamed of myself. How could I face my family, my friends, my co-workers or even the physicians I called on? I remember bragging to everyone that I was going to be the youngest Salesperson of the Year at Allergan. That effort was the recurring excuse I made for not visiting my family more often or partying with my friends. And they all understood and supported me. I told them that when the year was up, and it was announced that I was Salesperson of the Year, I would throw a big party to celebrate the occasion.

How could any of them trust me or even believe in me after this? The way I surmised it, none of them would want to interact with a failure like me. That day, I went from looking at myself as God's gift to sales to looking at myself as a fraud. Nothing had prepared me for the fall I took. No book. No training program. Nothing I had ever read or been trained on taught me how to handle this. Even if they had, would I have listened? Probably not.

That afternoon I walked out of Denny's with a mindset and perspective that would ultimately set the tone for my second, full year as a sales professional.

Drowning In Guilt

I remembered 1997 as an endless charade to hide my shame and failure, and masking my guilt. It was the type of guilt felt when your promises or commitments are not honored. I had let myself down, along with everyone I cared about. I continued to work hard and make sales calls. I continued to work my territory as diligently as before. The big difference was that with each passing day, I questioned myself more and more. I had lost all confidence in myself and my abilities.

You know the slippery slope, the one that once you are on it, you are in for a long, arduous downward spiral? Well, I wasn't just on it, I had pushed the pedal to the floor.

If what I had been doing the previous year was not working, what was I supposed to do? Why had I failed? Why was life treating me so badly? I did what all of the sales training books said to do, and look what happened! I followed Allergan's training to the point that I was leading in all of the statistical categories, except the one that really mattered...sales results. I repeatedly asked myself, what does it take to be successful in sales. It wasn't long before my question turned from, "Why had I failed," to " Should I just quit?"

Nobody seemed the wiser about my inner turmoil, because the smile on my face and dressing the part hid my anguish. My attitude had turned from optimism and confidence to pessimism and self doubt.

STEP 6: Giving It Your All

At some point, in all of our careers or life in general we've allowed our egos to master us. Sometimes we're able to recognize our ego leading us down the wrong path and reel it in before it gets out of control. Other times, we are caught up in our own self-hype, living in denial until that one incident unexpectedly pounds us and our inflated ego into the ground.

This is the point in your story development when you honestly reflect on those moments in your career or your life where your confidence was shaken to its core.

Tip ➜ Start with identifying the point when you began to seriously question your abilities. To help you along, think of the times when you thought you did all of the right things to achieve a desired outcome only to realize that you weren't nearly as close as you thought you were.

Write those moments down:

_____

_____

_____

_____

_____

As you went through the process of digesting the reality of your situation and how your efforts didn't pay off, **write how this made you feel inside and the questions you were asking yourself**:

_____

_____

_____

_____

You just finished writing how you felt on the inside. You may remember, in my story, to this point, I was feeling lost on the inside, but outside I was putting on a wonderful act that fooled everyone but myself.

Now describe how you presented yourself to others during this period of your life. What attitudes of behaviors did you exude?

_____

_____

_____

Reminder ➜ Be sure to visit www.WhatsYourSalesStory.com/workbookcompanion to download the companion workbook. While at our site don't forget to share your sales story and check out the latest tips and techniques designed to help you become a perennial sales performer.

CHAPTER 3
How Your Manager Can Control Your Thoughts

*"If you don't know your story, you leave others to write
it for you. And their idea of a perfect ending
may not be in your best interest."*
~ Ja Marr Brown ~

"Ja Marr, you're burned out."

Those words will forever strike a nerve in me. Although my manager had said them nearly 10 years before I wrote this book, they will serve as a constant reminder of what I had gone through and where I was at that point in my life. That period is never too far from my thoughts as I remain acutely aware of just how much of a game of smoke and mirrors our ego can play on us.

> *By the time a salesperson gets to where they have lost their sense of purpose and direction, they're officially burned out.*

My initial thought as I sat across from my manager was, "How'd this guy know?" I thought I had done such a good job of hiding things that nobody would find out.

The meeting that produced his observation was a result of a conference call that had taken place two months earlier. To our team's surprise, our current manager announced that he was being transferred to a different division and that we were going to get a new manager, who was also on the call that day. Our manager wished us well and then hopped off the call in order to give Rick, the new manager, some time with his new team.

Rick previously had been a top-performing sales rep and had been promoted to sales trainer. He had a reputation in the company for being very blunt, no-nonsense, extremely competitive and all about the numbers. This became evident when one of the first things he told the team was, "If you are in the top 10 in the country, I do not care what you do; you can work one day a week for all I care. However, if you are at the bottom, well, let's just say that that is not an option. You either perform on this team, or you'll likely find yourself looking for a job."

I knew right then and there, it was only a matter of time.

The Price of Burnout

A cluttered mind cannot sell. By the time a salesperson gets to where they have lost their sense of purpose and direction, they're officially burned out. The problem is that most salespeople live in denial.

They simply keep doing the same things as they did before without realizing that they're confusing activity with accomplishment. That was me.

The thing about sales burnout is that it isn't just isolated with you. Burnout is like a virus. Once it infects one person, it can easily infect an entire team, oftentimes without warning. Burnout can kill a sales team, and a bad sales team can kill a company. The price to pay for being burnt out is steep, which I was about to learn.

When You're the Problem

After two months in his managerial position, Rick called me into his office for a one-to-one talk. He wasted no time and fired away with his first question, "Ja Marr, do you still like your job?"

Puzzled, I answered, "Yes, I still like it."

Rick didn't leave any room for ambiguity and got right to the point. "Look, I'm going to be honest with you. I don't think you like your job. In fact, I think you want to be doing something else."

I totally was caught off guard and didn't know what else to say other than, "What?"

"Ja Marr, you're burned out."

I was stunned as I sat there digesting what he had just said. In one of those moments when your inner thoughts seamlessly flow from your head and out of your mouth, I said, "I'm only 22 years old. How in the world could I be burned out?"

"Ja Marr, it's ok to admit that you are burned out and want to do something else. It happens to a lot of people," he said, matter-of-factly.

My initial shock had already given way to anger and resentment. I also realized that he was trying to get me to quit. Even though, deep down inside, his words stung, because I knew they were true, my ego was not about to let this guy run me out of my job.

"Ok, you want me to be honest? I will," I defiantly responded.

"I'm frustrated, because I'm working my ass off and not getting the support I need from this company. My territory is one of the toughest in the country. It has significant managed-care challenges, and Allergan is not willing to spend the money to acquire the resources needed to turn my territory around. I am doing my part every day to change things, but I can't do it alone. I lead the team in calls per day and details per call. I lead the team in resource utilization, and nobody knows the products better than I do. It isn't my fault that the territory is at the bottom. Besides, my previous manager told me that the territory always has been at the bottom and always will be. I was told that this would be an 18-month development assignment; I am ready to be transferred now."

Rick didn't hesitate with his answer. "Ja Marr I know that you work hard, but you are not effective. You are confusing activity with results. This is precisely why you are burned out. It has nothing to do with the territory or a lack of support. You're the problem. Even if I did place you in a different territory, which I am not, you still would be ineffective. You're just not good at sales."

Before I even had a chance to respond, he concluded the

meeting by placing me on verbal warning. I was told that if I didn't turn my sales numbers around that I would be fired. He opened a folder on his desk and pulled out a document. He turned it around and slid it across the desk.

"To document that you're on a verbal warning, you need to sign this. All it does is acknowledge that I have officially placed you on verbal warning."

You know those movies when you see the character sitting calmly across from someone. Then the next thing you see is him leap across the table at the person they're mad at. Only seconds later, you realize it didn't happen; it was only the director showing you what was going on inside the character's mind? For a brief moment, that was me.

While I didn't leap across the table at my manager, his words washed over me, bringing with them an avalanche of emotions, most of which I had never felt to that degree before. Let's face it, I'd never been told I wasn't good enough. Sure, my first manager said the LA territory was bad and always would be bad, but he wasn't criticizing my abilities. In this case, Rick clearly was saying that I was not good enough to work at Allergan. On top of that, now he wanted me to sign a document admitting it. Not only was this foreign territory for me, but as a fierce competitor, my natural instincts were to stand up and fight back.

"I'm not signing that," I declared.

"Ja Marr, it doesn't really matter whether you sign it or not, because what we spoke about here still applies. All this is doing is acknowledging that you heard and understand what we discussed."

After what seemed like an eternity of silence, I chose, instead, to stand up, and without uttering another word, stormed out of his office. As I walked through the rows of cubicles and side offices, on my way out of the building, I found myself experiencing a strange contradiction of feelings.

On one hand, I noticed the people working at their cubicles and in their offices. I couldn't help but wonder, what the hell do these people have on me? My immediate conclusion: NOTHING!

I reminded myself of passed achievements: Whittier College Student Body President, dean's list, basketball team captain, numerous sports awards, the lead in calls made, and presentations delivered, etc. Not only does my manager not know or appreciate the talent that I have, he and Allergan don't deserve me.

If this company didn't want me, I would take my talents to a company that did.

Yet, at the same time, I was curiously unable to look anyone directly in the eye as I moved through the office. The part of my enormous ego that believed that I could do no wrong was still in the driver's seat. However, there was no mistake; doubt was beginning to erode my confidence.

I stormed out of Allergan's headquarters, whatever doubt that was growing inside me would have to wait. By the time I reached my car, I had made my decision: If my manager wanted me to go, I would leave on my own terms. If this company didn't want me, I would take my talents to a company that did.

STEP 7: Signs of Burnout

Burnout can disguise itself as personal problems, bad territory, bad sales collateral, illness, etc. While common sense will tell you that your efforts are 100% your responsibility, the reality often is that the more burned out you become, the more your ego shifts the focus from you onto others. The result is that you begin to take on less responsibility for your efforts and results.

Burnout is very much like a virus. Once burnout infects one area of your life, it tends to creep into multiple areas. As I alluded earlier in this chapter, once burnout invades one member of a sales team, it can quickly spread to kill the power of the entire team.

On the following lines, describe a time in your career or your life when you were burned out. Be sure to write down the signs of pressure and burnout that you experienced?

_____

_____

_____

Next, write out how you disguised your burnout, and if or how it affected those you worked with or interacted with outside of work.

_____

_____

_____

How long did you overlook your burnout, and what did it cost you both personally and professionally?

_____

_____

_____

STEP 8: The Power of Another's Words

In this chapter, you read about how my manager's perception of me intensified my situation. You also saw early on in the book how my first manager's perception of my territory fueled my desire to prove to him and others that I could single-handedly turn it around.

Now, it's your turn to write the part of your story (career) when your abilities were questioned.

How did you feel in the moment you were told your skills, efforts or abilities weren't good enough?

Tip #1 ➜ Your abilities may have been questioned by a manager, teacher, coach or friend etc. Think about how the words and actions of others have made you feel, both good and bad, and the impact this has had on your career and in your life.

Tip #2 ➜ As you write your answers down, it's important to keep in mind how your ego responded to these situations when they occurred?

_____

_____

_____

Reminder ➜ Be sure to visit www.WhatsYourSalesStory.com/workbookcompanion to download the companion workbook. While at our site don't forget to share your sales story and check out the latest tips and techniques designed to help you become a perennial sales performer.

CHAPTER 4
Searching for a Way Out

"When you blame others, you give up your power to change."
~ Douglas Noel Adams ~

"Tell me about your success at Allergan," the local district manager (DM) asked.

I had received a tip from one of our competitors; they were looking for a sales rep in the LA territory. Rather than dismiss this opportunity, as I would have done at any other time in my career, I thought it was the perfect opportunity to stick it to my boss.

I answered the DM's question by playing up my production levels and how I led my team in several key statistical categories. "I have led the team in calls per day and details per call. In addition, I have held the most number of dinner programs, and I'm also the lead person on the team in terms of clinical-product training."

He smiled and said, "I'm impressed. Usually reps this new to pharmaceutical sales rarely lead their teams in all of those categories, especially in clinical-product training."

I was feeling pretty good about things at that stage of the interview. Then, the DM asked me a question that I wasn't prepared to answer and, truthfully, was hoping to avoid.

"With all of that productivity, you must be one of the top performers at Allergan. What's your current sales ranking?"

I sat there for what felt like several minutes, wondering how I could spin this answer in my favor. I didn't want to lie, but I also knew that the truth did not bode well for me. Never mind the rankings, I told myself, I've got a stellar background. I just haven't been given a fair chance to let my talents blossom. I answered with confidence, couching my response with details of how I'd outperformed other veteran reps on my team and how I felt my talents would greatly enhance their company's efforts in LA.

"How's your relationship with your manager?"

I did my best to remain positive by saying that it wasn't the best, and at times, I felt he had held me back from reaching my full potential.

He then asked me how I expected to improve my sales results if I was working in the same territory, and if a new boss would really make that much of a difference in my performance?

Here were more questions that I wasn't prepared to answer. In my mind, I had been so consumed by the desire to get out of Allergan and stick it to my manager that I missed the irony that my current bad territory was exactly the same territory I was interviewing for with my competitor.

I gathered myself, and in my naivety, answered, "For one, the products I would be selling are different; Secondly, I would be working for a boss who supports me and believes in my potential. And finally, being in a culture that is more conducive to my style would help me to reach my full potential. All of these things would go a long way in making me a top performer at your company." Sounds like reasonable answers, right? The reality, however, was that my ego impeded my ability to recognize that the DM actually was testing me to see if I would take any responsibility for my current situation. I didn't see it at the time, but my ego was clearly still in the driver's seat.

The interview ended well – or so I thought, and I left feeling confident. I knew that with a new company, new boss, new products and overall change of scenery that I would rise to the top very quickly. I fully prepared myself for the official offer and was ready for a fresh start.

Two weeks passed before I received the call from the DM. Assuming I had the job, I asked "When do I start?"

"Ja Marr, I want to thank you for your patience and for taking the time to interview. Unfortunately, the position has been filled by a more qualified candidate." He went on to say that he would keep my resume on file, and if another position opened up, they would call me.

Frustrated, hurt and feeling lower than low, I found myself unable to contain my internal thoughts and emotions.

"You know what? If you cannot see the value in hiring me right now, there's no need to keep my resume on file. Don't bother calling me back." And with that, I hung up.

I sat there in my apartment, a heightened sense of anxiety and frustration building to a crescendo. My boss didn't believe in me. My customers didn't seem to trust me. My competitors didn't want me. That day marked the beginning of the end as I took a self-guided tour into what I now refer to as *professional depression.*

STEP 9: What Do You Care About?

Take this moment to think about what is most important to you when it comes to selling, and answer the question: **What Do You Care About?**

Don't underestimate the importance of this simple question. At first glance, it might seem really simple to answer. This is one of the most important steps in mapping out your story. Be as honest as you can be and really stretch yourself by going beyond a surface-level answer.

Tip ➔ As you write your answer, consider the role it plays in your daily sales efforts. *On what level does your answer affect, positively or negatively, your actions in the field and at home? How does your answer affect your customers?*

_____

_____

_____

Reminder ➔ After you've completed this step, read the following section of this chapter, and then come back to your answer. See if you have a different perspective. This step may be one that you will revisit as you delve deeper into my story and your own.

The Secret to Becoming a Great Salesperson

After the rejection from my company's competitor, I slept-walked through my job for the next several months. Every morning, I had to pump myself up just to get out of the front door. The psyche job I had to do would only last for a short period of time. By the end of each day, I was mentally, emotionally and spiritually exhausted.

Sure, I did a great job of masking what I was feeling on the inside as I kept up the charade for everyone around me. Internally, though, I was lost, confused and sinking deeper into a depression that I did not want to take responsibility for.

Ever since my father gave me Dale Carnegie's, *How to Win Friends and Influence People*, I had turned to books as a source of knowledge, guidance and inspiration. From books on sales, leadership and biographies and even to random books of fiction, no matter where I was in life, I always could find the answer I was looking for within the pages. Now, for the first time since my father had placed Carnegie's book in my hands, I couldn't bring myself to read, let alone look at a book.

To drown out the reality of my situation, I partied too much, drank too much and essentially did whatever I could to numb the pain. During that period, I started to believe what my manager had said. Maybe he was right, and the pharmaceutical sales industry was not the job for me. Worse yet, maybe I really didn't have what it took to be a good salesperson.

"You have to care about something more than making money and getting promoted if you want to be successful in sales."

I started to explore alternative career opportunities. There was the idea to open a new restaurant. I figured, what better way to control my destiny than to be an entrepreneur, my own boss. I interviewed several restaurant owners and managers and soon realized that the restaurant business was not right for me.

Hollywood Dreams

For as long as I could remember, I had had an affinity for the entertainment industry. From talk shows and movies to music and radio programs, I always have been interested in the creative aspect of entertainment. With my existing career seemingly going nowhere, I figured this was as good a time as any to indulge my passion.

First, there was radio. I toured several local radio stations and interviewed on-air talent, station managers and salespeople. Although I found radio to be interesting, it did not feel like the perfect fit for me.

Next, I shifted to television, where I had had some previous experience. In Hollywood, success sometimes comes down to who you know, and I knew one of the most powerful sales managers in the business, my former boss at KTLA (television station), where I had interned for a semester during college. I gave him a call, and he said he'd be more than happy to make some introductions but wanted to meet with me first.

A week later, we were reminiscing like old friends. At one point during our meeting, I asked, "What is the secret to becoming a great salesperson?"

Suddenly, the vibe in the room changed: He was sizing me up, looking past my question and seeing the truth behind my façade. Earlier pleasantries aside, he looked at me with a steely glare and asked, "Ja Marr, what do you care about?"

A simple question, but I honestly had no idea how to answer it. In all the training programs I had attended and sales books I had read, I never had been asked that question. Stumped, I mustered the only response that came to mind, "I care about getting promoted as fast as possible and making as much money as I can."

He leaned across his desk; his look was unsettling, "You're a liar. I don't believe you when you say that you only care about getting promoted and making money."

Defensive, I fired back, "I'm in sales. If I don't care about those things, how am I going to be successful?"

He looked me straight in the eyes and said, "You have to care about something more than making money and getting promoted if you want to be successful in sales. And until you find out what that is and are not afraid to say it, you will fail. Don't forget, Ja Marr, buying and selling is emotional. The secret to being a truly great salesperson is that you have to understand and be in touch with your deepest emotions and those of your customers. Until you know what you care about and genuinely care about your customers, you will not be successful."

I didn't get it. Instead of digesting what he said in a way that would propel me out of my depression, I felt offended and dejected. Even though he gave me the phone number of a vice president of sales (VPS) at FOX television studios, I couldn't pull myself together to take advantage of the lead. My ego had been hit once again, and I left his office more disillusioned than before.

STEP 9: What Do You Care About? (REVISIT)

You now have had a chance to see not only how I initially responded to the question, "What do you care about," but you also have read how the answer was first conveyed to me.

With that in mind, go back and revisit your answer for Step 10. As you review your original answer, do you now have a different take on it, or is your perspective still the same?

Despite the downward spiral my career and overall mindset was heading, I still felt that the only way out was to continue to pursue a career in entertainment. Since I did not follow up on the lead I had been given, I decided to break into the television industry my own way; by developing my own public-access television show.

I was certified through the City of Torrance Public Access Television department and became a "Television Producer." Along the way, I met Matt Owen, who also was seriously pursuing a career in television. Matt's focus was to become a comedian, and I had aspirations to be a talk-show host. It seemed like an ideal pairing, and we teamed up to produce a couple of full-length shows and a number of smaller segments. We called our show, *The Variety Show*, to represent our combination of comedy and serious issues. You can see a clip of our show at (www.whatsyoursalesstory.com/gallery)

My confidence returned to a level I hadn't felt in nearly a year. The success I found with the shows reignited my passion and unleashed my creativity. Because of how focused Matt and I were with the shows, I cut out the heavy drinking and partying that had started to consume my personal life. There were problems in paradise, however, as our full-time jobs had prevented us from producing more shows, and we were not making any money. Reality set in, so I shelved the idea of being a television producer and talk-show host.

Hitting Rock Bottom

My state of mind and outlook at Allergan had not improved, so I continued to bounce around dozens of ideas for new and more fulfilling careers. Each one, I soon realized, would require going back to school for an MBA. With what confidence I had left, I applied and along with 40-plus aspiring MBA students, was accepted into the Riordan Fellow's program, which is a seven-month MBA preparatory course at University of California Los Angeles (UCLA) (www.riordanprogram.com).

I completed the Riordan Fellow's Program, took the GMAT and applied to three business schools, all of which rejected me.

How had I gone from being a student body president, on

the dean's list, MVP of sports teams and INROADS intern, full of life and optimism, to a dejected, untalented and unwanted professional? Those are the thoughts that started to consume me.

I was at a loss. I was selling in an industry I had no desire or talent to be in, working for a company that, I believed, had no faith in me. Every idea I had had for a way out fizzled. No matter how unlimited my opportunities may have been at Allergan, I couldn't see them anymore. I had been searching for a way out of my problems and came up empty.

My options had run out, and my spirit was broken. The way I saw it, I had nowhere to run and nowhere to hide. I finally had hit rock bottom.

STEP 10: Hitting Rock Bottom

Every sales professional will experience some form of struggle or self-doubt during their career. For some, it may last a couple of days, whereas for others, it can drag on for months, eventually causing one to hit rock bottom. Rock bottom can represent different things to different people. For the purpose of this exercise, let's look at rock bottom as reaching a place in your career where you are burned out, and you feel there are no options for you.

If hitting rock bottom happens to you, make no mistake, the effects will be felt in your personal life just as much as they will at work. In many cases, your personal life starts to suffer even before your sales career.

While hitting rock bottom is not guaranteed for every sales professional, the possibility that it can happen is real. But just because it can happen and does happen to thousands of sales professionals every year, does not mean that it has to happen to you.

This is the point in your sales story development where you address hitting a major roadblock in your career. Perhaps you hit an emotional rock bottom in your sales career. If it hasn't happened in your career, describe a time in your life where you felt that you had run out of options and that life had thrown you too tough of an obstacle to overcome.

Tip ➜ This step isn't about how you got yourself out of the situation but what you felt like during it. For now, I want you to be more in tune with how you felt during this period of your career or personal life. This step is about writing out what happened during that period of your life and the circumstances surrounding it. How did you feel emotionally?

_____

_____

_____

_____

_____

_____

Reminder ➜ Be sure to visit www.WhatsYourSalesStory.com/workbookcompanion to download the companion workbook. While at our site don't forget to share your sales story and check out the latest tips and techniques designed to help you become a perennial sales performer.

CHAPTER 5
Letting Go & Letting In

*"If you wish to see the truth, then hold
no opinion for or against."*
~ Osho ~

I was living a lie.

Outside of my boss, no one else in my life knew that I was struggling at work. And nobody, including my boss and family, knew the personal hell I was living.

The old saying, "Never let the truth get in the way of a good story," was my mantra during that period. I told family, friends, customers and even my colleagues, the same story: Everything was great; Ja Marr was doing just as well as he always had. To the outside world, I had a well-paying, flexible job with a company car and an expense account. I was living the dream. But knowing the truth of my situation coupled with the lie I was telling everyone was hurting me, and it was tearing apart my career.

> As strong as my ego was, it was not equipped to properly handle the obstacles I faced.

Gaining Control of My Ego

My ego had grown over the years as my confidence was reinforced by my personal success. My confidence had pumped up my ego and had been the basis of my determination in the face of adversity. However, as strong as my ego was, it was not equipped to *properly* handle the obstacles I faced.

I cannot stress enough that during this period of my career, my daily sales efforts were driven by my ego. Unfortunately, it was an ego that was out of control.

Of course I knew what was happening to my career and the lie I was living, but my ego would not allow me to express the truth of my situation to those around me. People wanted to hear that everything was fantastic, and I wasn't about to disappoint them.

The one thing that I couldn't escape was the fact that the main source of my frustrations at work were coming from my manager. I was consumed with the idea that he hated me and was bent on firing me. Being on verbal warning only made these fears more real. Outside of how this translated into my personal life, the truth is it had a very real impact on my ability to sell.

When I was in the field, I wasn't thinking about what was important to my doctors or their patients. I wasn't even thinking about what was most important to me. Everything I did in the field was driven by paranoia and fear about losing my job. I knew that if I got fired, the charade I was playing would be found out. Ja Marr officially would be a failure.

While my confidence took one hit after another, my ego went into protective mode, prompting the lies I fed others about who I was and what I was achieving, to the lies I fed myself about who really was responsible for my efforts. No matter the reality of the situation, my ego protected me. In turn, my productivity and ability to perform at the level I was capable of suffered. I did not see this at the time and therefore was not able to get it under control when I needed to.

There is a lot to be said about the importance of one's ego in sales. You need to have one. But it needs to be managed.

My ego was holding me hostage, and it became increasingly more difficult to do my job effectively. I was so afraid to make a mistake that I became pensive and passive. No outside-the-box thinking. No extra push.

When it came to answering phone calls or email, I was like a victim in a horror movie—afraid to look under the bed or open the door for fear of what was there. I was certain that one of those calls or emails was my manager's official notice that I had been canned.

> *There's a lot to be said about the importance of one's ego in sales. You need to have one. But it needs to be managed.*

Just Do Your Job

One of the eye-care physicians I called on had invited me to attend the grand opening of his new medical office. Despite the fact that I had very low market share with his practice, I had agreed to support the event by sponsoring the food.

I arrived feeling uncomfortable, knowing I had gone out of my way to help cater food for a physician who barely gave me any business. To make matters worse, my direct competitor in the territory was there, and I don't believe he offered any support (beyond his presence) to the event despite the fact that he had the lion's share of the physician's business. I felt totally used. To further my pain, there were more than a dozen other eye-care physicians in attendance, none of whom I had any level of market share with.

I nervously and painstakingly mingled with a few physicians but was rapidly approaching the point where I could no longer put on the act. I became overwhelmed with emotions, ranging from anger and rejection to being played for a fool and, ultimately, sadness. Feeling unable to hide my emotions, I decided to leave quietly. Just as I was walking out the door, a doctor approached me. I knew of him, but he was not one of my current targets.

To this day, I do not know why I opened up to the degree I did, but before I knew it, I was divulging everything I had been going through. And I mean everything—from the fact that I disliked my boss, and he was about to fire me, to my failed attempts to leave Allergan and that I felt like a fraud to my family and friends. I even talked about how I felt used by the doctor whose party we were at. I had been unable to tell the truth to anyone, family, friends or even myself. Yet, here I was unloading my baggage to a physician I barely knew.

The floodgate had been opened, and I was past the point of lying anymore. It felt really good to let out the truth. I noticed a disinterested look cross his face, as if he were annoyed by what I was saying. It didn't matter; I kept talking. He had had enough, though, and finally cut me off. In a distant, unemotional tone, he asked, "Why are you spending so much time worrying about your job and your boss?"

"What? I don't understand." I said.

"Instead of worrying about your job and what others are thinking, why don't you just do your job? You're not giving your best. But if you were and still got fired, well, then at least you would know you had done your best. At the end of the day, your best is all that matters. Worrying about everything else just gets in the way of what you're supposed to being doing."

As I stood there, digesting his words, he hit me with two more questions. "Have you tried to learn everything you can from your job? Have you tried to learn anything from your experiences?"

He didn't care if I could answer the questions or not and glanced at his watch. It was clear that the conversation was just about over.

"If you are going to get fired or leave a job, it is better to leave knowing that you gave it your best shot and that you tried to learn everything. That way, you are better prepared for the next phase of your career. Remember, every time you think something is coming to an end; something new is about to begin. The real question is whether you're ready for it or not." Then he walked off. No handshake. No well wishes. Nothing, or so I thought.

It took a moment for me to collect my thoughts. I had just unloaded my feelings onto a potential customer, and instead of feeling awkward, I felt a sense of relief. It was cathartic. For reasons I did not understand at the time, his words resonated with me. Walking out of the party, I felt an immediate change in my perception of my situation.

Driving home that evening, the realization that I had spent so much time worrying about being fired and protecting my ego finally hit me: My fears had interfered with my performance, that it was my responsibility and no one else's finally made sense.

That physician had come into my life, unexpectedly, at just the right time. Had I met him earlier in the evening, there is a strong likelihood that I would not have opened up as I did. It was at the precise moment he approached me that I found myself no longer capable of lying.

His words forever changed my life and put me on a path towards excellence. That evening marked the last time I focused on what my manager thought of me. I realized that I was projecting my personal issues onto him, instead of owning them myself. The problem wasn't my manager. It was me and my out-of-control ego.

The following morning became the first day of the rest of my career.

STEP 11: Where's Your Focus?

Steps 11 and 12 mark a pivotal point in writing your story. On the lines below, answer the following questions.

1. Describe a time in your career or life when your focus on something negative prevented you from being at your best. **In what ways did that affect you professionally or personally?**

_____

_____

_____

2. **What is it - RIGHT NOW – that you are focusing on that's preventing you from excelling at your current job or in a certain area of your personal life? What do you quietly fear or lament over? What are your current frustrations?**

_____

_____

_____

STEP 12: Unexpected Insight

As was the case in my story, many times in life, when we least expect it and when we are at our lowest point, someone appears and offers the insight that starts our healing process. It could be a total stranger or someone we know. It can even be a passage in a book or scene from a movie.

1. **Describe a moment in your life when this has happened to you. How did the person come into your life? What was it that they said that had such a profound impact on you?**

_____

_____

_____

2. Now look at your current sales career. No matter where you are in your career, more than likely, there are areas you can improve on.

With that in mind, choose the one person whom you have the utmost respect for and imagine what kind of advice they would give you to improve your sales efforts right now.

_____

_____

_____

Reminder ➜ Be sure to visit www.WhatsYourSalesStory.com/workbookcompanion to download the companion workbook. While at our site don't forget to share your sales story and check out the latest tips and techniques designed to help you become a perennial sales performer.

CHAPTER 6
I Am Talented

"If you can't believe in yourself, no one else can either."
~ Deacon Jones ~

My new-found perspective, focus and attitude was about to be put to the test.

Because I no longer was worried about what my manager thought of me, I was in a much better frame of mind on the day he rode with me in the field. Rather than being focused on impressing him, I was intent on impressing the doctors I was calling on.

I was no longer worried about my boss, but the reality of my situation at work remained the same. I was still at the bottom of the rankings. I knew I had to get a handle on the answer to the question that continued to burn inside me, "How do I become consistently successful at sales?"

Cocky, Assumptive and Aggressive

From day one, my manager had touted himself as a seasoned and successful salesperson, and he had the President's Club hardware to back it up. Like most of the reps on our team, I believed him and looked forward to watching him in action and learning.

I was so wrapped up in what was important in my own world that I failed to see what was important in my customer's world.

Our first stop was one of the biggest accounts I was trying to win business from but had not been successful in moving any market share with. The way I figured it, if I had any trouble with this doctor, having someone with the sales caliber of my manager certainly would help. Worst-case scenario, I'd at least get to learn something about becoming consistently better at sales.

No sooner did we enter the doctor's practice than I began to see just what kind of salesperson my manager was: cocky, assumptive and aggressive. While I had not been able to get anywhere with this doctor and his practice, I knew one thing for sure, this call was not going to help. In fact, my manager and the doctor quickly engaged in a verbal argument.

During the argument, I went through what some people call an out-of-body experience. No, my spirit didn't float above the room, but as my manager was doing all of the talking, I was in a unique position to notice things with this doctor that I had completely overlooked when I was the one delivering the presentation.

I felt uneasy about how things were progressing between my manager and him. They were debating issues that were irrelevant to the doctor's needs. The doctor said things directly but implied his needs non-verbally. When I had called on him previously, I was so wrapped up in what was important in my own world that I failed to see what was important in his. Now, here I was for the first time clearly recognizing the needs of this doctor.

A Big Win

By observing the interaction between my manager and the doctor, I now saw exactly how we could help this customer. Even so, I was hesitant to cut off my manager and step in. He was supposed to be the expert salesperson, and I was the guy on verbal warning. But the situation was getting further out of control, and I felt compelled to take action.

My new-found focus and confidence were on full display as I first calmed the doctor down by speaking to him in a respectful and more measured tone. Then I referenced several key points he had just made to my manager and anchored those to what he had told me about his practice previously. The stark contrast between my style and my manager's dramatically changed the doctor's mood and earlier resentment was replaced by receptivity. He began to listen intently as I acknowledged each one of his needs.

When I had finished, he informed me that it was the single, best presentation by a pharmaceutical rep he ever had witnessed. He not only approved the proposal that I had presented, he signed it on the spot. The doctor turned to my manager, and said, "You can learn a lot from Ja Marr...He gets it." Then he turned and walked away.

Leaving the doctor's office, I wasn't thinking about how I may have impressed my manager nor was I relieved about finally winning the business from a big account. For me, it was a validation of the profound shift in my mindset and overall outlook, both in sales and in my personal life.

Despite that very big win, and of course, outshining my boss during a pivotal presentation, I knew that there were many more questions to answer. The first one was how in the world was it possible that I, literally on the verge of being fired, outperformed a more seasoned and knowledgeable sales professional, who also happened to be my boss?

Being Right vs. Being Successful

During the short walk to the car, my manager said nothing. I could tell he was irritated, and I couldn't blame him. For a guy who had professed to be so proficient at sales, he had come off more like a used-car salesman.

Once we got into the car, he congratulated me on the call. I wanted to gain his perspective on what he thought I had done well, so I asked him. Rather than answer me, he went into a tirade about how unprofessional the doctor's staff was and how rude the doctor was to both of us. Shifting responsibility?

As he was going on about the doctor's attitude, I could not help but think he just did not get it. Our job as salespeople is not to force customers into submission or win arguments. Our job is to demonstrate how our products and services can best meet their needs. In the case of the doctors, those needs extended to staff and patients. We need to listen, hear their stories and then relate to them by showing we understand and can help them achieve their goals.

> *Our job as salespeople is not to force a customer into submission or to win an argument. Our job is to demonstrate how our products and services can best meet their needs.*

I vividly remembered many of my past sales calls. Most of the time, I talked more than listened and tried to force-feed my product info to uninterested doctors. I thought about the many situations I had employed the "show-up-and-throw-up" method. Why? Simple, I was trying to make 10 calls a day and cram as many details as possible into a two-minute-or-less presentation. How many times had I cut doctors off in mid-sentence just to make my point? Most of all, I remembered all of the arguments and debates I had won and all the sales I had lost in the process.

Those realizations further validated my new-found sense of confidence and focus. However, the feeling that I was better or that I had outperformed my manager in a critical sales call was not an ego boost. For the first time, I truly felt I was talented at sales. No false sense of security. No hype or trumped-up enthusiasm. No bravado. I truly felt, in my heart, a sense of confidence that I never had experienced in my career. Now, I just had to fully understand exactly what I had done in that sales call and learn how to replicate it.

An Unexpected Discovery

That night, after my day in the field with my manager, I was more determined than ever to build on the momentum I had created. Not surprisingly, there seemed to be more questions than answers as to how to accomplish this. There was no doubt in my mind, though, where I would need to go to find them.

I returned to the place that had provided answers to so many questions throughout my life – books. Not since my initial struggles with my career had I even thought of reading any of the books I had accumulated over the years. But if I were to understand how to replicate my recent success, I had to reinvigorate my mind and continue reengineering my perspective on sales as well as in my personal life. And there was no better place to do that than in books.

I approached my bookcase, scanning the various rows for, *How to Win Friends and Influence People*. When my dad first handed me that book when I was 12, he said the lessons in it would help me get through any situation so long as I applied them. I always had found Carnegie's timeless wisdom useful, and so it seemed like the most logical place to start. It had been so long since I had approached the bookcase that I didn't remember where the book was. I must have looked through each row twice before I finally located it. But as I reached out to grab it, another one unexpectedly caught my attention. It was a book on the world of manufacturing.

To this day, I cannot fully explain why I reached out and took hold of that book over Carnegie's, other than initial curiosity. As I fixed my eyes on the title, I barely remembered reading the book, let alone why I had purchased one on manufacturing.

I noticed right away that one page in particular had been dog-eared, so I opened to it. Every book that I ever had read was marked up with handwritten notes, Post-Its and a healthy dose of a yellow highlighter, aids to help me truly understand and remember what I had learned.

However, on the page I opened to, there were no hand-written notes, only a slightly faded, yellow highlight over one word – KAIZEN. Seeing it brought back a vague recollection of the term, and I remember being intrigued by it but obviously not enough to do more than simply highlight it for future reference.

Before long, I found myself sitting on the sofa, where I spent the next several hours reading it from cover to cover. This time, I was highlighting the word KAIZEN as well as every paragraph that described or referenced its philosophy.

Taken from the words 'Kai" (continuous) and "Zen" (improvement), KAIZEN is a Japanese term that means continuous improvement. Some people translate "Kai" to mean change, and "Zen" to mean good or for the better. The book revealed how that concept transformed the Japanese economy after World War II. Also, the philosophy paved the way for a revitalization of many American companies as they began to implement Kaizen and similar principles in their manufacturing organizations.

I looked beyond KAIZEN's relevance to manufacturing and immediately saw how it could be applied to my career and life in general. I was hooked, and my life would be profoundly altered as a result of my exposure to KAIZEN.

> *Taken from the words 'Kai" (continuous) and "Zen" (improvement), KAIZEN is a Japanese term that means continuous improvement.*

The KAIZEN Philosophy

While the book provided a starting point for a fundamental understanding of the KAIZEN philosophy, most of it related to manufacturing. Finished with the book, I transitioned to the Internet where I spent the rest of the night and into the early morning hours researching everything I could find on KAIZEN.

I learned that although KAIZEN had been successfully applied to the world of manufacturing and other areas of life, rarely had it been used in sales, sales management and leadership. From that night on, I would spend the better part of my professional life redeveloping this centuries-old philosophy to fit today's multifaceted and ever changing modern world. I placed the emphasis of my work on KAIZEN in the area of becoming a perennial sales performer, corporate leader and how it can help fulfill one's personal life.

After hours of researching, note taking and contemplating, I devised what would become an adaptation of the definition of KAIZEN. The adaptation was based on three core principles:

*(1) **Continuous Improvement:** Focus on improvement every day as opposed to being overly focused on the end result. Making small changes can lead to major improvements.*

*(2) **The Relentless Pursuit of Excellence:** Define your idea of Excellence (to live according to your purpose and who you want to be), and relentlessly pursue it every day.*

*(3) **Eliminating Wasteful Thoughts and Behaviors:** Understand that every thought and action either takes you closer to or further away from your "Excellence." Eliminate any thought or action that does not take you closer to your "Excellence."*

Eliminate Waste

In rapid succession, three completely separate incidents had profoundly changed the direction of my career and life. There would be more incidents to come, but my discovery of the KAIZEN philosophy combined with the win that I had accomplished while with my manager and the recent discussion I had had with the doctor at the party, all served as a collective awakening for me, and set me on a path toward excellence.

In the days following my exposure to KAIZEN, the why and how behind the struggles in my career had become clearer than ever. When people struggle, they grasp at straws. Instead of utilizing my strengths and what made me successful, I deviated from the path of perennial success. I allowed my ego to take over and was headed in the opposite direction of where I had envisioned I would end up.

I rediscovered the importance of looking within myself for answers as opposed to searching for them in outside things. To rid myself of the destructive nature of my actions and thoughts, I decided to initially focus on the KAIZEN principle of *Eliminating Wasteful Thoughts and Behaviors.*

In my research about KAIZEN, I came across the word Mudas, a Japanese term for waste. Waste can come in the form of thoughts and behaviors. In manufacturing, Mudas is applied to the efficiency of the assembly line by making small changes that equate to major positive returns and eliminating wasteful actions that slow down or disrupt efficiency.

The Japanese, and eventually, American manufacturers, learned that making dramatic, sweeping changes in order to affect change, almost assuredly brings about wasteful activities and takes much longer to achieve a desired outcome. I knew that order to make the adjustments necessary to improve my sales results; I needed to first eliminate the wasteful thoughts and actions that had been holding me back.

STEP 13: Maximizing Talents Through KAIZEN

To realize that I not only possessed the talent to sell, but to rebound from the lowest point in my life and rediscover my talent was a truly special moment in my life.

It is easy to forget that you're talented and lose your belief when you are dealt one obstacle after another. But when you are able to move past the obstacles and finally see a clear path, knowing you have what it takes to travel that path is an awesome feeling.

The KAIZEN principles have been used in many areas of life and business to enhance and elevate talent. With that in mind, step 13 in developing your sales story will focus on identifying what it is you're talented at and how to utilize the KAIZEN principles to fully maximize your talent.

(A) **Write down whatever you feel are your special, unique talents. Go beyond selling and explore all of your talents.**

_____

_____

_____

(B) **Next, write down all of your talents in the area of selling. Now rank them in terms of importance to your current responsibilities at your company.**

_____

_____

_____

(C) **Take your list of talents and determine where they can be further utilized as it relates to the following three KAIZEN principles:**

Continuous Improvement:

_____

_____

_____

The Relentless Pursuit of Excellence:

_____

_____

_____

Eliminating Wasteful Thoughts and Behaviors:

_____

_____

_____

Reminder → Be sure to visit www.WhatsYourSalesStory.com/workbookcompanion to download the companion workbook. While at our site don't forget to share your sales story and check out the latest tips and techniques designed to help you become a perennial sales performer.

CHAPTER 7
Responsibility

*"Whatever you fight you strengthen and
whatever you resist persists."*
~ Eckhart Tolle ~

No longer questioning my abilities and even with my confidence steadily rising, I was still a long way from reaching my full capacity of talent. During this period, my reality was that no matter how much confidence I had in my talent, I still firmly believed that the territory I covered, coupled with the lack of support and guidance from my manager, was going to be my biggest set of obstacles to rising in the rankings.

"No matter how you try to pass the buck, at the end of the day when it comes to your performance, whose responsibility is it?"

Two weeks following the ride-along with my manager, he called to inform me that his boss, the Vice President of Sales (VPS) at Allergan, was going to ride along with me during an upcoming day in the field. Whether it was myth or fact, the overriding belief with the sales reps at Allergan was that if the VPS rode with you, it meant you were now officially at the point of being fired. Accepting that belief as the truth, I knew it was going to be a pivotal day in my career.

Let's face it, armed with a new philosophy and mindset that I had adapted from KAIZEN, coupled with some nice wins in the field, I was moving in the right direction mentally and emotionally. As far as my manager and his boss were concerned, I was still on the chopping block due to my poor rankings.

Despite my growing confidence, I was nervous about being with the VPS for an entire day, especially because of what I thought it meant for my job. The recent success I had had with my own manager, however, better prepared me to handle the pressure. As I had done with my manager's ride along and in keeping with the KAIZEN principle of *Eliminating Wasteful Thoughts and Behaviors*, I realigned my focus. I would not waste my time or efforts worrying about impressing the VPS, or even try to save my job. Instead, I would shift my focus and actions to impress the doctors we were going to call on.

Taking Ownership

We weren't in the car for more than 10 minutes, and already the day was getting off to a bad start. The VPS immediately began to grill me about my poor sales performance.

Instantly, everything I had been trying to instill in my mind with the principles of KAIZEN was forgotten. I went on the defensive. I reiterated what was told to me by my hiring manager: The LA territory was one of the worst in the nation; it always had been and always would be. Of course, the VPS viewed the situation completely different. He was steadfast in the belief that the problem was me.

I went on with my version of reality and stated that in addition to the bad territory, I had no support from my current manager. I even talked about my recent ride along with him. I retold the story of how I had to save the sale myself, and added that after my manager's behavior, I am at least as good of a salesperson as he is, maybe even better.

"How is he going to provide me any sense of guidance or selling support when I'm the one who had to save a sale he was screwing up," I asked. "My production and effort is better than anyone else's on our team, but my numbers still are bad. Until I get better support or placed in a better territory, I don't see how things are going to change."

"Ja Marr, let me ask you something," the VPS said. "No matter how you try to pass the buck, at the end of the day when it comes to your performance, whose responsibility is it?"

I knew what he was trying to do, but I was not about to give in. In my mind, he was trying to get me to admit that the poor sales performance was my entire fault, and that would give him enough HR ammunition to fire me. To outsmart him and not dig my own grave, I stubbornly continued to present my version of the truth. I repeated my earlier answers about the bad territory and lack of support. To his credit, the VPS was not about to give in, either.

He narrowed his focus, and with a stern, yet measured tone, stated, "It's your responsibility. Nobody else's but yours. Everything that happens in your territory, good or bad – is your responsibility. You have talent, but you have failed miserably at taking ownership and owning up to your responsibility. Until you do, you will not be successful at Allergan or any other company."

Our debate ended right there. Not because I immediately understood his point, but because I had nothing left to use in my defense. For the next 30 minutes, we drove in total silence to the first appointment. I opened up my mind and allowed his words to percolate. Something about the line, "…you will not be successful at Allergan or any other company," resonated. Perhaps, that was why I had not been able to secure any meaningful way out of Allergan for the last eight months. My perception of what was actually possible in my territory, and the meaning behind taking ownership and responsibility, started to actually sink in.

We pulled up to the office of our first physician. Before we got out of the car, the VPS turned to me and once again asked, "So whose responsibility is it?"

"It's my responsibility," I confidently replied. For the first time in my career, I had understood what it meant. A clear sense of relief came over me.

The VPS recognized the importance of this and simply replied, "Good. Now I can teach you how to improve your sales results."

Without the burden of anger, resentment or frustration

hanging over me, I walked toward the physician's office with a sense of relief. Despite all of my new-found beliefs and improved mindset toward *Continuous Improvement*, I reminded myself that there still were important lessons to be learned, and I just learned a big one. As a result, a major turn in my career had taken place.

STEP 14: Ducking Responsibility

On the following lines, discuss a time when you either knowingly or unknowingly followed your ego in the wrong direction and ducked responsibility.

Tip → Perhaps you're avoiding taking responsibility right now in your career, so answering this may not be easy. To that point, this step in developing your sales story is one of the hardest for many people, because it requires complete honesty.

Identify, on the lines below, where you have ducked responsibility in your career or personal life:

_____

_____

_____

(A) Now that you've identified where you are avoiding responsibility, detail who you blamed or what you pointed to as the reason you failed to achieve your desired outcome.

_____

_____

_____

STEP 14: Ducking Responsibility (continued)

(B) Describe the moment when you came to the realization that your "state of affairs" was your responsibility. Who or what played a role in this realization?

_____

_____

_____

(C) Detail the impact, positive or negative, when you finally decided to take responsibility for your situation.

_____

_____

_____

(D) If you haven't taken responsibility for your current situation, what changes in your life or performance would occur if you were to reverse this thought process?

_____

_____

_____

Reminder → Be sure to visit www.WhatsYourSalesStory.com/workbookcompanion to download the companion workbook. While at our site don't forget to share your sales story and check out the latest tips and techniques designed to help you become a perennial sales performer.

CHAPTER 8
When The Sale Is Not Enough

"You can make more friends in two months by becoming interested in other people than you can in two years trying to get people interested in you."
~ Dale Carnegie ~

Due to his extremely high volume, the first doctor we called on was someone that was on my top five list of targeted physicians. I didn't have a lot of market share with him, but the potential to ramp up sales was extremely high. Because of the potential, I decided to have the VPS take control of the call. Like the ride along I recently had with my manager, I was eager to see him in action and learn.

Right away, I was taken aback by his technique. Not because I was impressed, but because I was so annoyed. Rather than speed up our time to speak with the doctor, he made small talk with each person he came across in the office: two patients who were in the waiting room, the girls at the front desk, nurses and the office manager. I couldn't believe what I was witnessing.

I kept thinking, "I am trying to turn my career around by eliminating wasteful actions and thoughts, and here's the VPS deliberately wasting time." I was on the verge of being fired for a lack of sales performance, and I couldn't understand why this guy was in here, "shaking hands and kissing babies," like a politician on the campaign trail.

Since he was the VPS, I gave him the benefit of the doubt and anxiously waited to see how he would position our products to the doctor.

To my utter amazement and shock, the first thing he did was ask the physician a series of questions, all of which seemed completely irrelevant to me. In fact, he barely mentioned any of our products. "That is not selling," I thought to myself.

We left the office; I felt cheated and embarrassed. It was extremely difficult to get face time with that particular doctor. As

> *"How can you expect to be successful in sales if you don't know what your customers really are all about?"*

a matter of fact, the only reason he had agreed to a meeting was because of the VPS' attendance. It was a perfect opportunity for the VPS to leverage his position and get the doctor to commit to prescribing more of our products. Instead of taking the opportunity to sell our products and gain a commitment for usage, I felt he had taken a major step backwards with the account and ruined my only chance with that physician.

Who Your Customers Really Are

The moment we left the office, the VPS began asking questions about the physician we had just seen. "Do you know where he went to school?"

I honestly didn't know whether to laugh or ask if he had lost his mind. Knowing my job was on the line, I made the wise choice of doing neither and simply replied that I didn't know.

Relentless, he rattled off the following questions: "How many children does he have; what are his hobbies; do you know what his long-term plans are for the practice; does he plan on opening an additional office, or is he looking to retire soon; and how long has his staff been with him, and what are their hobbies?" I was completely dumbfounded! Besides being unable to answer any of them, I thought they were totally irrelevant.

Overcome by sheer exasperation, I blurted out, "What do any of those questions have to do with selling?"

As we got in the car, he simply asked, "Do you feel like we wasted our time with the doctor?"

"Yes. Yes, I do. He could have been one of my biggest volume doctors, and I expected you to position our products, so that we could increase our business with him. I just don't see how anything you talked about with him had anything to do with sales. You barely even mentioned our products, let alone close him for more business."

"Let me ask you something, Ja Marr. How can you expect to be successful in sales if you don't know what your customers really are all about?"

Once again, my ego spoke, "I do know my customers. I know them very well. I know that they have patients with needs, and we have the products that can meet those needs. Isn't that the most important thing? If I didn't know the doctor, how could I have gotten the business I currently have?"

Undaunted, the VPS said, "Getting the sale is not enough. Look, I don't know what you have talked with him about in the last year, but I have no doubt anyone could have gotten the same amount of business out of him as you have. And I am equally sure that if you had taken the time to really get to know him and his staff on a personal level, you would have achieved quite a bit more success with his practice."

My grip on the steering wheel tightened as my level of frustration grew. No support from my manager, and now, the VPS even questioned the success I had achieved!

"Sales is not about simply telling doctors what you want them to hear," he went on. "It is about understanding them as business people and as individuals. If you truly know the needs and wants of your customers, and apply your knowledge to what is important to them, they will respond to you in a very positive way."

"But I do understand their needs and wants," I countered.

"Seriously, Ja Marr, how can you say that and not be able to answer any of the questions I asked you about him? Remember, every day, every person who doctors come into contact with wants something from them. Patients want to be seen faster, and they want their problems

> *"Successful selling is not about you. It's about your doctors, their staff and the patients they serve."*

solved. Their staff wants more money. And every day, at least a half a dozen or more pharmaceutical and medical device reps from different companies come calling, and they all want the doctors to use more of their products. If you can be that one rep who allows his customers to express their needs, and you communicate with them genuinely, then you will be consistently successful."

Naturally, my ego didn't want to hear that, but it did make sense. Even so, I still was not completely convinced.

"But what does the number of children or their hobbies have to do with prescribing our product," I asked.

"When I talk about their needs, Ja Marr, I'm not just talking about their needs as it relates to the success of their practices, but their personal needs as well. Don't forget, they have personal lives outside of work, too. Think about how your own personal life affects your success at work, or how your success at work impacts your personal life. Successful selling is not about you. It's about understanding your doctors, their staff and the patients they serve."

And that's when it hit me. I remembered how much of a relief it was for me to have talked about my personal issues to that unsuspecting physician at the doctor's grand-opening party. If anybody understood the impact work had on personal life, it was me. The most ironic realization for me was that I recognized how my perception of my manager's lack of support affected me, so I could only imagine how the doctors must feel.

For the first time in my career, I actually stopped long enough to understand that everyone they meet during the day is seeking support from them. I thought about what my VPS had just said and wondered how many sales reps encountered by the doctors and their staff on a daily or weekly basis were genuinely interested in supporting and getting to know them? The principles of KAIZEN, as they applied to sales, crystallized.

Getting the Sale Is Not Enough

Prior to the ride along with the VPS, my perception of my job, and sales in general, was that it was all about presenting the features and benefits of your products and then closing as hard as you could. I had to make the sale, which, for us, meant we had to "gain a commitment" from the physician; otherwise the call would not be successful. The VPS not only taught me the importance of taking responsibility, but he helped me draw a direct correlation between selling and the KAIZEN principles. A major step towards sales excellence, I realized, is that getting the sale is not enough.

If I truly wanted to improve my numbers, I would need to reengineer how I perceived selling. I would begin by *Eliminating Wasteful Thoughts and Behaviors* in regards to my interactions with doctors and their staffs. While this sounds like something you would learn in sales 101, it is very easy for sales professionals to get wrapped up in our own challenges and desires, so much so, that we forget who and what is really important in the sales process. It not only takes us further away from achieving our desired outcomes; it alienates us and our companies from the very customers we're trying to connect with and sell to.

With KAIZEN, the *Relentless Pursuit of Excellence and Continuous Improvement* are a byproduct of *Eliminating Wasteful Thoughts and Behaviors*. I realized that the VPS hadn't wasted time by making small talk with the office staff and doctor; he was building a bridge between our company's products and us with everyone inside the doctor's practice. What I had been doing, which was putting more emphasis on my agenda while ignoring the staff and doctor's personal and professional needs, was truly wasting time. My earlier efforts not only created more distance between me and the doctors, they further pushed me away from realizing my full potential.

The Transition

From that day on, I made it a top priority to build truly remarkable relationships with my customers. My interpretation and efforts behind the KAIZEN principle of *Continuous Improvement* was centered on getting to know the doctors and everyone in their offices, better. My intention with each call shifted from simply trying to sell my product to genuinely get to know everyone, no matter their titles or positions. My sole focus was to make everyone I encountered feel like the most important person I had met with that day.

> *I was not the star. Allergan's products were not the stars. The doctor, their patients and their staff were the stars. It was my job to put the spotlight on them and treat them as such.*

I won't say that this realignment of my mindset and actions was easy. Prior to this new approach, I was under the false impression that the only person that mattered was the senior decision-maker such as the physician. And they only mattered in so far as how much product they agreed to take. In my short career, I had ignored the staff, not really thinking they were important. The only time I would speak with the staff was to get to the doctor.

To make the transition from struggling to a *Relentless Pursuit of Excellence*, I had to take another big step toward shrinking my ego. To most of the doctors and their staff, I was an egotistical, young punk in a nice suit. I had been. Now, however, I was determined to change their perception of me. But first, I had to change my perception of them.

I was not the star. Allergan's products were not the stars. The doctor, patients and staffs were the stars, and it was my job to put the spotlight on them and treat them as such.

Am I Getting Fired?

Upon the conclusion of our ride along, I dropped the VPS off at the airport. Before he exited the car, I had to ask, "So, am I getting fired?"

He looked at me and replied, "Whose responsibility is it for the success or failure of this territory?"

"It is my responsibility," I repeated my answer from earlier in the day.

"Are you going to truly get to know each of your accounts and the people in them? And most importantly, are you going to make their success more important than your own?"

I confidently answered, "Yes, I will."

For the first time that day, he smiled and said, "Now you are ready to learn something. Because of that, I am not going to fire you. As a matter of fact, if you commit yourself to what I taught you, I may even promote you one day." And with that, he shook my hand and headed toward the airport.

STEP 15: Defining Your Relationships

The lesson I learned about relationships has been one of the most important in my career. When you want to make a sale, it is very easy to lose sight of who and what is truly important in the sales process.

Contrary to what many salespeople think, it isn't how well your product works, the value it delivers to your customers or how quickly you can close a sale. Each of these are important, but to place more emphasis on them than you do in getting to know who your customers are will only prolong the sales process and hinder your growth as a sales professional.

With that in mind, step 15 is one of the more important steps in developing your story. Think about relationships you have with three of your customers.

STEP 15: Defining Your Relationships (continued)

Write the name of your top customer:

_____

Write the name of a customer you would like to get more sales from:

_____

Write the name of one "lead/prospect" you would like to secure as a customer:

_____

Now define each of them as people. To help you with this, consider the answers to the following questions.

1. How is what you do emotionally relevant *(professionally & personally)* to each of these individuals? Remember, each are at different places in your sales cycle, so the connection with you and your company will be different.

_____

_____

2. What are the most important "desires" these three want to experience as it relates to your product's solution? Is it different for each one or the same for all?

_____

_____

3. What are the primary challenges or "pain" they want to avoid as it relates to your solution? Is it different for each one or the same for all?

_____

_____

4. Are any of these individuals married? If so, what are the names of their spouses? How long have they been married? When are their anniversaries?

_____

_____

5. Do they have children? If so, how many and how old are they? Do you know their names?

_____

_____

6. What day and month are each of their birthdays?

_____

_____

7. What hobbies are they most interested in? Are any of these hobbies related to your company or solution?

_____

_____

Reminder ➜ Be sure to visit www.WhatsYourSalesStory.com/workbookcompanion to download the companion workbook. While at our site don't forget to share your sales story and check out the latest tips and techniques designed to help you become a perennial sales performer.

CHAPTER 9
The Return of the Ego

"Ego takes everything personally."
~ Eckhart Tolle ~

Intent on placing the spotlight on the doctors and their staff, I arranged for a Perceptorship with one of the doctors I had been calling on. A Preceptorship is when a person shadows a physician or any other professional to learn from them. Essentially, it is like a mentorship.

The doctor I was set to spend the morning with was Dr. Clark. He ran one of the most successful practices in my territory and was someone I had worked hard to build a relationship with. It was not an easy relationship to build. In preparing for the Perceptorship, I recalled some of my earliest meetings with him. Most of the interactions between us centered on his request for more samples and my repeated requests for him to prescribe more of Allergan's products; neither one of us would give in.

But like many of the doctors I had spent time with over the past two years, I had placed too much emphasis on myself and Allergan's products. In order for me to continually improve as a sales professional and raise my numbers, I needed to truly get to know him and his staff.

On this day, I was focused on achieving that outcome.

Dressing for Success

One thing I had noticed on previous calls was that Dr. Clark never wore suits. He seemed to prefer either polo-style or button-down dress shirts and slacks. Not wanting to come off as an "arrogant punk wearing a suit" and hoping to make a favorable impression, I, too, wore a polo-style shirt and slacks.

When I greeted him, the first thing he said was, "What are you doing dressed like that?" I thought he was joking and asked him what he meant. He suggested that I go home, and put on a suit and a tie. The exchange took place in front of seven of his staff members. They weren't the only ones, however, who heard it. There was a large, open glass window at the front desk, so every patient in the jam-packed waiting room could hear our discussion. I looked to his office staff to see if I was missing something, but they wore the same stunned expression as me.

"When you come into my office, you always need to be buttoned up and professional. We'll continue with this Preceptorship when you are dressed properly," he said.

I defiantly shot back, the anger in my voice unmistakable, "I don't get this. Every time I visit your office, you're wearing a casual shirt and slacks. How can I be dressed unprofessionally when I am dressed the same as you?"

Surprisingly unfazed by my tone, he explained his reasoning, "Ja Marr, this is my practice. I have earned the right to wear what I want. But when you or anyone else comes into my office for professional purposes, I expect you to show respect for me, my staff and patients by dressing appropriately."

Then Dr. Clark grabbed a patient chart, reviewed it and glanced at his watch. As he motioned for his nurse, he stated, "I do not have any more time for this, Ja Marr. If you want to come back like a true professional, feel free. If not, it was nice knowing you, and good luck on your career," and walked away.

I stood there, confused, angry and utterly embarrassed. Left with no other choice, I turned to leave. Unfortunately, there were approximately 15 patients between me and the door. Most of them had heard the verbal lashing I just had received. Even though I was unable to look at them, I just knew they were staring at me. The short walk through the waiting room felt like one of the longest in my life.

Me, Mom and My Ego

I got into my car and was so furious and confused by what had just transpired that I pounded my fists against the steering wheel.

I spent several minutes running through scenarios in my mind. They ranged from going back into Dr. Clark's office and telling him off to wondering why I had been tortured like that. I couldn't help but think of all of the changes and progress I recently had made, which included my new approach. None of it mattered, now, because I was still getting kicked in the ass.

Too angry and depressed to work the rest of the day, I drove home. On the way, I made the decision to write my resignation letter. Once I got home and started writing it, the emotions I had been feeling overtook me, and my eyes welled up. The realization that this was officially the end of my sales career was extremely tough to face. Before I emailed the resignation letter, however, I decided to come clean.

I thought about calling my grandfather, who always had been my closest confidant. But I realized I would have to divulge everything that had been happening, and I couldn't bring myself to tell him the truth and let him down. I thought about calling my father, but my ego kept telling me to be my own man. Even though I knew my ego was misleading me, I still followed it. The only other person in my life who I could count on to tell me that everything was going to be alright and give me some positive encouragement was my mom. I picked up the phone and called her.

Like my grandfather and everyone else in my life, in the previous grueling months, not once did I tell my mom anything but positive things about my career. While I didn't get into the dirty details of my situation at Allergan, I did explain what had happened with Dr. Clark.

After listening to my story, she asked, "What if you change into a suit and go back? What's the worst that can happen?"

I replied, "Mom, this guy hasn't even agreed to do business with me for a year, and I wore a suit and tie every single time, except today. What would be the difference if I went back? I'll tell you; he probably would have even less respect for me! Going back would be a win for him!"

My mom's tone changed to one that I remembered as a kid, when she would do away with pleasantries and get right to the heart of a situation. "You are too focused on yourself and your ego, instead of being focused on how you best can work with him. It is his office, and you are trying to do business with him. At the end of the day, all that matters is whether or not you get the business. You need to act according to the way he does business."

I couldn't believe my mom, of all people, was taking Dr. Clark's side. Exasperated, I raised my voice and said, "Mom, I called you for support, and you're telling me that I should go back and do what he says? Look, I did try and do business the way he does, and guess what? Dr. Clark embarrassed me in front of his staff and patients, and then kicked me out of his office. There's no way I'm going back." I couldn't believe I had just yelled at my mom and figured she was about to really let me have it.

> *"Son, you're letting your ego get in the way of your success."*

She did, but not in the way I was expecting. She saw right through me and calmly said, "Son, you're letting your ego get in the way of your success."

She was absolutely right. But, once again, it was not what I wanted to hear.

"I gotta go," I snapped and abruptly hung up.

I was filled with a mixture of emotions, all of which were swirling so fast in my head that I had to stand up. I spent the next several minutes angrily pacing my apartment. Several questions filled my head, like the following: How could my mom turn on me; how am I going to explain to friends and family that I no longer work for Allergan; and will mom accept my apology?

I didn't have the answers and, quite frankly, was too exasperated to even try to find them. None of the positive changes I had made seemed to make any difference, and now, on top of that, I had yelled at and hung up on my mom. I sat back down at my computer and re-read my resignation letter. Just as I was going to email it to my manager and VPS, I hesitated, again. What if my mom was right? Of course, she was right. Now, what was I planning to do with her suggestion?

The words, *"Don't let your ego get in the way of your success,"* played over in my mind. I was reminded how my ego always had been the culprit, tripping me up throughout my young sales career. From the issues with my boss and being a young, cocky and arrogant sales rep, to ignoring the importance of getting to know people and getting pissed off at Dr. Clark. Every obstacle I had faced, the way I handled the setbacks, they all came back to my ego getting in the way of my success.

First things first, I needed to call my mom back. I apologized profusely for my angry tone and rude behavior. I also thanked her for, once again, being the greatest mom and friend in the world. I expressed my admiration for her as well as my appreciation for telling me the truth about myself. Thankfully, she accepted my apology and urged me not to waste anymore time before heading back to Dr. Clark's office – wearing a suit and tie this time.

Getting ready, I imagined how much success I could have achieved if I would have recognized sooner just how much trouble my ego caused me. Rather than get bogged down in "what could have been," I knew I would not allow that to happen again. The light bulb had finally gone on, and I was not about to turn it off!

Swallowing My Pride

Two hours after I had been told to leave, I pulled back up to Dr. Clark's office. Before I got out of the car, I took a deep breath realizing the enormity of the situation.

It didn't matter what Dr. Clark's reaction would be. I knew

that in order for me to achieve any level of success, I had to get my ego under control. It had tripped me up long enough and returning to his office was a major step for me, personally and professionally. Knowing that, however, didn't make the walk to his office door any easier. I was extremely nervous, but I swallowed my pride and went in, my head up and looking as confident as I could.

As I walked through the waiting room, I was thankful and relieved that all of the patients, who had heard my earlier exchange with Dr. Clark, were gone. I sheepishly approached the front desk and announced I was back to see Dr. Clark for the Preceptorship.

Three staff members were behind the counter, including the office manager, who smiled and said, "Ja Marr, I'm proud of you. I don't think I would have been able to come back. I'll go get Dr. Clark."

While she was gone, the other two staff members looked at me and then glanced at each other. They both seemed anxious to see what was going to happen in round two. I was anxious, myself, and had no idea what to expect.

When Dr. Clark emerged, flanked by the office manager and his nurse, I braced myself for another lashing. I could only imagine what the issue would be this time. Wrong color tie. Shirt not properly pressed. Wrong style of or maybe my shoes weren't polished enough....

In the midst of considering what bad things could befall me, I had mentally prepared myself: No matter what happened, there was absolutely no way I would let my ego get in the way of my success, this time. If told to leave, I would return, again and again, until I figured out how to connect with him and gain acceptance as a

That morning marked a turning point for me as a person and as a sales professional. It was the first time I had gotten control of my ego and didn't allow it to get in the way of my success.

valuable part of his team. Imagining the worst, I braced myself for another lashing. What did take place, though, I would never have imagined.

"Ja Marr," Dr. Clark said, smiling, "The fact that you came back tells me more about your character than anything you can tell or sell me about your products. Because of that, I am going to commit to giving your products a fair evaluation in my practice. If the outcome proves to be as good as the data you have showed me in the past, then I will convert to your products."

I'm not an actor and could not hide the astonished expression on my face. He reached out, shook my hand and concluded, "Now, let's get going with that Preceptorship," then motioned for me to follow him.

As I passed by his staff, I noticed that each of them smiled at me, and the office manager even patted me on the back and said, "Congratulations."

The events of the morning marked a turning point in both my career and life. It was the first time I had gotten control of my ego and didn't allow it to get in the way of my success. It also started a long and fruitful relationship with Dr. Clark. As promised, my products received a fair evaluation. Eventually, he became one of my highest-volume customers.

STEP 16: Swallowing Your Pride

Write about a current situation in your career where your ego is getting in the way of your success, and how you can swallow your pride and put the spotlight on your customer. You also can choose a situation in your personal life when you decided to let your ego make decisions for you.

Describe the situation?

_____

_____

_____

How can you improve the situation with the customer and overcome your ego by placing the spotlight on him instead of you?

_____

_____

_____

Reminder ➜ Be sure to visit www.WhatsYourSalesStory.com/workbookcompanion to download the companion workbook. While at our site don't forget to share your sales story and check out the latest tips and techniques designed to help you become a perennial sales performer.

CHAPTER 10
Knowing What You Want

"The greatest things all have an elegant simplicity."
~ Deacon Jones ~

My success with Dr. Clark gave me some assurance that I was on the right path. But I didn't want to get too caught up in the end-result and lose sight of the KAIZEN process or the progress I was making with my improved mindset.

In the weeks following my Preceptorship, I kept up my journal and listed the personal and professional growth I had made:

- I realized that the KAIZEN principle of *Relentless Pursuit of Excellence* is to focus on and be committed to the process of being successful, not just the success itself
- I understood the importance of *Eliminating Wasteful Thoughts and Behaviors.*
- I realized that every action or thought either takes you closer to or further away from your goals and aspirations in life.
- I constantly took stock of my ego and made every effort to not let it get in the way of my success.
- I stopped searching for a way to leave my problems, and I faced them head on.
- I focused on *Continuous Improvement*, which moved me to take full responsibility for my sales numbers. My goal was to try and get better every day.
- I ceased to blame the territory, my manager or other outside forces for my lack of success.
- My relationships with customers improved as I placed the spotlight on them and not on me; I was getting to know their staff on a much more genuine and personal level.

Everything Had Improved But...

As I finished the list and reviewed it, I couldn't help but feel a sense of pride and accomplishment. I eagerly anticipated the upcoming rankings and knew that with all of the strides I had made, it would show in my numbers.

I was determined to improve my rankings, but I also was cognizant of doing it the right way, by implementing the KAIZEN principles.

To my utter amazement, the email I received with the updated, 1997 rankings had me ranked 93 out of 98. The overall number of salespeople had decreased from 140 in the past year, due to layoffs. To this day, I have no idea how I survived those layoffs, but I did. And now, here I was, still sitting at the bottom despite all of my improvement.

Frustrated, I had asked myself, "What else do I have to do to be successful?"

Frustrated? Yes. Discouraged? No. I set out to put my new mindset and improved-skills to use. I was determined to improve my rankings, but I also was cognizant of doing it the right way, by implementing the KAIZEN principles.

What Do You Want?

The day after receiving the updated rankings, I set up a meeting with Dr. Smith, a customer who had opened an office in my territory after my initial struggles to manage my ego. With a better understanding of how to do that and armed with the KAIZEN principles, I had applied my new approach, truly getting to know customers, to Dr. Smith and his staff. However, despite my best efforts, my market share with him and his practice barely moved. Rather than get discouraged and point the finger, as I would have previously done, I decided to figure out why my new approach had not generated better sales results.

Dr. Smith was a shinning example of a doctor with whom I

felt I had a great relationship. But like many of the doctors I called on, he gave the lion's share of his business to my competitor. I wanted to discover, from his perspective, why he and other customers were not giving me much business even though I had vastly improved as a salesperson, and many of them had said that my products were at least as good as my competitors.

Entering his office that morning, I received a very warm welcome from every member of Dr. Smith's staff. Before speaking with him, I spent several minutes chatting about family, weekend plans and other unrelated, office topics with several front-office personnel. This type of welcome and interaction had become more customary as I had changed the way I connected with both the staffs and doctors I visited.

When I reached Dr. Smith's office, he and I spent the first five minutes discussing family and personal interests. Nothing about products or business was even brought up.

Dr. Smith was the first to get down to the reason behind this morning's meeting. "You sounded so serious over the phone, yesterday. I know that your reason for coming in is certainly different than your usual visits. So what is it you'd like to discuss, today?"

"I need to ask you something, and I want you to be brutally honest with me." He nodded his head, and I proceeded to outline my progress as an individual and salesperson.

"What I cannot seem to put my finger on, though, is why most of my customers remain uncommitted to doing business with me. The reason I wanted to sit down with you is that I trust your opinion. You've regularly told me that I am a great sales rep and how your staff loves me. You also have said that no other rep is as committed, knowledgeable and dependable as I am. Additionally, you think my products are great, and you have mentioned on several occasions that neither you nor your staff can stand my competitor."

Throughout my discourse, Dr. Smith smiled and nodded his head in agreement. "So, if I am truly that great and my competitor is really that bad, why do you prescribe more of his medications and do more business with him than with me?"

A few seconds of silence passed between us. Then, Dr. Smith unfolded his arms, leaned in and with a serious, yet warm tone, he said, "Ja Marr, the answer is simple. Yes, it's true my staff and I enjoy your visits, and you are the best rep that's ever called on this office. In fact, the staff especially loves how you know all of their names and are so dependable. And I have to commend you for giving great presentations and knowing your stuff inside and out. But that is where the problem begins."

> *"You present your message and tell a good story, but I have never once heard you ask for anything."*

He paused. I was literally on the edge of my seat, eagerly anticipating where he was going with this.

"You present your message and tell a good story, but I never once have heard you ask for anything."

My eager anticipation of his answer quickly dissipated and without realizing it, my ego had jumped into the driver's seat, again. "What? I don't understand. I always tell you what I want. I am closing for more business every visit."

"You might think you are, but honestly, Ja Marr, you're not."

I'm sure Dr. Smith could tell I was irritated, but he didn't let it get in the way of what he was trying to convey to me.

"Look, I'll give you an example. Take your competitor, for instance. This guy comes in like a bull in a china shop. I don't think he's once said hello to any of my staff, let alone asked them about their families. As soon as he sees me, there's no time wasted with small talk, and he always says what he is going to do for me and my practice and how easy he is going to make it for me to prescribe his company's products. And, at the end of the day, he follows through on exactly what he tells me he is going to do. As you know, I run a very busy practice, and although I am not a big fan of his, he makes it a little easier for me to run my business."

I leaned back in my chair, my energy and interest in hearing more had dissipated.

Dr. Smith's tone changed as he offered me what could best be described as a lifeline, "As I said before, you're great. You're respectful. You're professional. But, Ja Marr, we just don't know what you want, and I certainly don't know how you're going to make it easy for my practice to transition from your competitor's products to yours."

He leaned back in his chair, assuming the posture he had had earlier, his arms folded, again. His eyes were intently trained on me, as it was now he who awaited a response.

In the few short seconds it took to collect my thoughts and allow for what he said to percolate, it all started to make sense. As tough as it may have been for my ego to take, I instantly retraced my interactions with Dr. Smith and my other doctors and realized he was absolutely correct. I was simply presenting a lot of information but not asking for the business. Oh, I thought I was, but my ego's perception of what was happening and the reality of the results and perception of my doctors told an entirely different story.

I nodded my head and couldn't help but smile. Dr. Smith told me exactly what I had needed to hear, and I was in the right place mentally to hear it. Mindful of the time we had spent, I stood up and confidently said, "Dr. Smith, based on our relationship, and the fact that you believe in my products, I am going to tell your staff that you are switching all of your business over to my products and that you will not be utilizing my competitor's products from this point on. I will personally work with your staff to make this transition simple and easy on you, your staff and your patients. Do you have any questions?"

I decided that if I could not openly ask my customers for their business, regardless of how friendly we were to each other, it was not a true relationship.

Dr. Smith smiled, reached out and shook my hand. "No questions at all. And, Ja Marr, I am glad that you asked."

Earn the Right to Ask for the Business

The eye-opening visit with Dr. Smith allowed me to see how I was hesitant on directly asking for the business, because I was afraid if I did I would ruin the relationship with him. The irony of that belief is that not only did I not have as good a relationship with many of my customers, as I had thought, but I also was afraid of the answer they would give me.

What if they flat out refused? Then what? How would I go back in to get their business, and what would I say to them then? Most importantly, had I even earned the right to even ask for their business?

Early in my career, my mindset for sales had been wired too tightly around the idea that sales is all about closing. We were taught that the harder the close the better. I closed for business without having properly developed the relationship and earning the right to ask for the business. When that didn't work, I tried developing relationships without focusing on closing.

I assumed that by developing "relationships" and presenting my product information in elaborate detail, it would naturally get me more business. The customers not only didn't get it, they were not fully convinced I was even asking for the sale, let alone clear on what I was asking for at all.

My understanding and perception of what a true relationship is with customers dramatically shifted after my meeting with Dr. Smith. I realized that a solid relationship existed when there is mutual trust and respect on both sides, and you have the lion's share of the business. I decided that if I could not openly ask my customers for their business, regardless of how friendly we were to each other, it was not a true relationship. In essence, I had to earn the right to ask for their business.

The difference this had on my sales calls and my relationships with doctors was dramatic. Because I had an initial foundation built with many of my doctors and their staff, there was not a huge climb that needed to be made in order to earn the right to ask for their business. I simply needed to feel comfortable enough to ask for it and understand what this meant for them. This made it easy for my doctors to move to my products by minimizing the cost of changing products and vendors.

I accomplished this by coordinating the change with the entire office. Each staff member, from the part-time personnel to the office manager, knew precisely what was taking place. By diligently and closely working with them on the protocols and procedures, everyone was on the same page, and a smooth transition was made.

The key to all of this was getting to know each customer personally and knowing how each office worked. This allowed them to make the transition to my products seamlessly and painlessly. Of course, it also had a profound impact on my sales numbers. My overall approach to selling and building long-standing relationships had forever changed.

STEP 17: Asking for the Business

Step 17 in the development of your story will most assuredly be an ego- stretching exercise. It should also redefine how you view "closing" and relationships.

Asking for business is an essential component of being successful in sales. Even so, it goes without saying, every single sales professional, at various stages of their career, have left untold amounts of business on the table simply because they didn't "ask for the business." Worse yet, there were customers who were turned off, because you asked for the business but hadn't earned the right to do so.

The reasons behind not asking for the business or rushing for the sale can range from fear and insecurity to a lack of experience or multiple other causes. Regardless of the reason it happens, unless you can reach the point of knowing why you're asking for the business and are able to leverage your relationship with your customer to confidently ask for the business, your success in sales will be more by accident than by design.

A. How do you feel after a sales call when you know you should have asked for the business but were afraid to? Describe these feelings.

_____

_____

B. What can you do to improve your relationships with customers and earn the right to ask for their business, at the right time, every time?

_____

_____

CHAPTER 11
When the "How" Meets the "Why"

*"You can achieve the most satisfaction when you
feel related to some greater purpose in life,
something greater than yourself."*

~ Denis Waitley ~

Heading into October 1997, I was riding a wave of success, which, less than a year earlier, would have seemed impossible. The events of the past several months, starting from divulging my situation to a random physician to the priceless insight of my mother and Dr. Smith, would serve as the connection points for my personal and professional turn around.

Had I not paid attention to these events and their importance to my career, it's a safe bet you would not be reading my story. Moreover, had I not been present to my own situation, it is more than likely that my career, my potential and overall life would have taken a strikingly different path.

Putting those lessons to use, coupled with an innate desire to improve as a salesperson and as a man, steadily increased my sales. For the first time in years, I felt connected to my customers and more importantly, I felt connected to who I was as a person.

Mom, Can We Keep Him?

Seven years earlier, I was in Jr. High School and had just finished doing my homework when our doorbell rang. Standing on our porch was a five-year- old boy, named Billy. I recognized him as one of the foster kids who lived with a family a few houses down. My friends and I would pass the young boy and his siblings playing outside but, due to the difference in ages, I never paid much attention to them.

Billy didn't waste any time and told me that his family's dog had just given birth to litter of puppies. Unfortunately, he explained, his family could not take care of all of them. He had given all of them away except for one and wanted to give the last one to me and my family. He turned around and lifted a puppy from a box behind him. I don't know what surprised me more, the fact that this kid chose our house or that I hadn't even seen the puppy behind him. Either way, my surprise gave way to an instant connection I had with the puppy. I knew right then that we had to give him a home.

For the next 20 minutes or so, Billy and I begged and pleaded with my mother to let me keep the puppy. "Mom, please, can I keep him? C'mon, mom, please?"

She called my father to the door, and he agreed to let us keep the puppy – but with some pretty stiff terms. For one, while the puppy would be our family's dog, he would be my sole responsibility. Any slip up in taking care of him meant he would be living under someone else's roof. I was more than happy to agree to the terms.

We named the puppy, Ceasar, and nearly every day for the next couple of weeks, Billy would come over and check on him. He and I would play with Ceasar in the front yard, and I began to learn about the young boy's story. My mother had told me that Billy was a foster child, but that didn't really mean anything to me until I learned how he had been given a home and a family when his biological parents could not take care of him.

Billy told me how the family that lived a few doors down from us had adopted him and another boy, and they had several foster children coming in and out of the home. While they weren't his biological parents or siblings, he made it clear that they were his "family."

His parents came over one day to pick him up, and they told my mother and me more about Billy's life and the lives of the foster children. I was overwhelmed by the depth of their compassion to give these children a home and a family. My relationship with

> *I decided that no matter where my life took me I was going to be a positive role-model for the foster children.*

Billy and his family grew from that day forward. I was so touched by what his parents were doing to provide a better life for these children that I decided: No matter where my life took me, I was going to be a positive role-model for the foster children.

My Promise

Through my teenaged years and up to my initial months at Allergan, I never wavered on fulfilling that promise. No matter how busy things got for me during high school, college and my internship at Allergan, I maintained a regular connection with Billy's family.

As we each grew older, I stood as an example for the foster children in my neighborhood and showed them that no matter where you come from, your dreams were never too far out of reach. It wasn't until things turned bad in my career at Allergan that my contact with Billy's family, not to mention my own, became inconsistent.

Throughout that dark period in my life, whenever I did visit my parents, Ceasar was a constant reminder of the promise I had made, and I was not fulfilling it to the degree I had imagined nearly seven years before. I'd see Ceasar, how happy he was to play, and I was compelled to walk over and check in on Billy and his family. Like everyone else in my life, I never let on how bad things were. To Billy's family, I was a living embodiment of the American Dream: Do well in school; get a degree; secure a great job; work hard, and anything is possible. On the outside, I played up this image, but inside I felt like a fraud. I'd surmised that any type of role model I hoped to be was nothing more than a smoke screen to my real-life disappointment.

A Painful Reminder

With things going much better for me at work and feeling more at peace with who I was, I decided to visit my family as well as Billy and his family on the first weekend in October. I really was looking forward to seeing everyone and, of course, playing with Ceasar.

Two days before that weekend, my mother called with the news that Ceasar had died. She said that he had become quite sick in the last couple of weeks. When they had taken him to the veterinarian, they discovered that he had terminal cancer, and even if treated, Ceasar still would have pain. My mother said she and my dad didn't want to burden me with this news, and they made the decision the day before to put Ceasar to sleep.

Since Ceasar had been put to rest at the veterinarian's earlier in the week, that weekend I returned home, we symbolically buried Ceasar. Now 12 years old, Billy stood next to me in my family's backyard, a makeshift memorial for Ceasar laid at our feet. I looked down at Billy and could see his eyes filling up with tears. I could not escape the thought or guilt of how many opportunities I had missed, over the last 18 to 20 months, to play with Ceasar and serve as the role model I had promised I would be for Billy and the other foster kids.

> *They looked at me for who I was, not who I pretended to be. I had lost sight of that in my pursuit of being the top salesperson.*

It didn't matter what I had gone through, who I was or what I did: Ceasar, Billy and the other kids never judged me. The sales numbers I hit or missed at work didn't matter to any of them. The number of sales presentations I made was irrelevant. Whether I got my doctors to move market share with products had zero bearing on their excitement when I visited. They looked at me for who I was, not who I pretended to be. I had lost sight of that in my pursuit to be the top salesperson.

While the loss of my dog was not easy on me, the emotional impact was not as bad as it would have been had it occurred several months earlier. I was in a better place mentally and emotionally, and my career was starting to get back on track. I put my arm around Billy and smiled at him. A critical element in my continued development was the realization that I had only shared with Billy and the other foster children the positive outcomes of my efforts, both personally and professionally. I could only imagine the struggles they had faced so far in their young lives. Sharing my challenges and the way I overcame them might have helped them realize that they're not alone, and provided a frame of reference for overcoming their struggles.

Walking away from Ceasar's makeshift memorial, I made another promise to myself. Never again would I let my ego get in the way of what was truly important in my life. It wasn't about being a big shot sales rep; it was about being true to who I was as a person and maximizing the opportunities I have had with those who mattered most in my life.

In order to fulfill the promise, I set out to help others, especially the foster children, and later in my career, sales professionals. Just as I had done, I wanted them to learn the importance of learning from and sharing their own personal stories. I did not want the foster children to think that they had to hide the truth about their struggles from me. I wanted them to know that I had struggled, too, and because of the struggles and how I chose to deal with them had made me who I am, today.

Losing a Mentor

The promise I made of not letting my ego get in the way of my success fueled my passion and drive to write this book: I wanted to share my story and, in doing so, inspire others to share their own stories. And that promise also inspired and motivated me at work. As a consequence, my efforts were finally showing actual results in the sales column.

My latest success came with a physician, who, only two months before, would not even give me so much as 60-seconds of his time. On this day, he committed to doing a 50/50 evaluation between my key product and my # 1 competitor's product. Not to leave anything to chance, I asked if we could call in Susan, his tech, and tell her what the plan was. He agreed, and everything was set.

The difference between what had been a non-existent relationship and a successful sale was the relationship I had been steadily building with Susan. She would later tell me that she had a real disdain for pharmaceutical and medical device reps, even me, at one time. When I dropped the attitude and started talking with her and the rest of the staff on a genuine level, such as calling each of them by name, and knowing and caring about their personal stories, she began putting in a good word for me with the physician. He trusted Susan and decided to finally give me more than a minute of his time. After establishing a relationship with the doctor and providing all of the clinical information he had requested, it was only a matter of time before that relationship blossomed into a win-win outcome for me, his practice and his patients.

After that successful sales call, I was pumped! On the way to my car, I must have smiled and said good morning to more than a dozen or so people, all of whom must've thought I was high on some wonder drug. I felt unstoppable. I knew I had a long way to go but to have made the leap I had up to this point only reinforced that I was on the right path.

While driving to visit another customer, my dad called. Since my earliest childhood memories, I always have admired and respected my father. Like most sons, it was important for me to do things that would make him proud of me. Even though my father had supported me and had been there for me throughout my entire life; once again, my ego had me convinced that he would only be proud of me if I was a success. My quest to do everything on my own, coupled with my oversized ego, prevented me from sharing with him what I had been going through since I graduated and joined Allergan.

Needless to say, when I received his call, I was excited, because I could finally tell him about my successes without lying.

I picked up the phone and enthusiastically said, "Hey, dad, perfect timing. You won't believe how great things are going. I just..."

He cut me off in mid-sentence. "Son, I need to tell you some bad news. Your grandfather passed away this morning."

It didn't register at first. "I'm sorry dad, I didn't hear you. What's wrong with my grandfather?"

"Son, he passed away. He died in his sleep. Your mom and I are heading over there right now."

Everything around me seemed to slow down. I felt a strange tingling sensation in my arms; my heart rate increased, and my breathing intensified as if I'd just finished a long, arduous workout.

"Ja Marr, are you ok," he asked.

"Uh....yeah...no...I...I don't know," I was stammering. "Can I call you back in just a minute?"

My entire family knew that my grandfather was my best friend, my confidant and my source of knowledge and insight. Throughout my life, I felt 100% at ease to confide in him and that he would provide me the advice I needed. During the last two years, however, as I hid all of my set-backs from everyone, he was the one person I really did my best to hide the truth from. If I felt 100% at ease confiding in my grandfather, why not tell him the truth? That cruel irony haunted me throughout my ordeal. It wasn't that I didn't think he could provide me the guidance I needed. It came down to the fact that I had convinced myself that out of all my family and friends, he would have been the most disappointed in me. I rationalized that I was protecting him. It reached a point that I was so ashamed for lying to my grandfather that I purposely avoided talking to him for more than a few minutes at a time, just so I wouldn't have to lie. I truly felt that I'd eventually right my ship, and everything would be ok. It never occurred to me that he'd pass away before I had the opportunity to say I was doing well and for it to be the truth.

And now, my grandfather, my best friend, was gone.

I hung up the phone and pulled over, stopping by the side of the road. I sat there and attempted to make sense of what my father had just told me. I couldn't; an avalanche of emotions rolled through me, and I sobbed uncontrollably for several minutes. I had never experienced such a loss or felt so helpless in all of my life.

My Potential

I took several days off from work, dividing my time between family and alone-time.

From the funeral to the gathering at my grandmother's home, I couldn't escape the guilt of lying to my grandfather, which also reminded me that I had lied to all of the people who meant the most to me. It got worse when everyone said how proud my grandfather was of me and how he would constantly talk about the wonderful things I was doing with my life and my career.

> *Never in his life did he think that giving up was an option, even in the most dire circumstances.*

My moral compass was out of alignment, and my guilt, compounded by grief, was overwhelming. Even though things had improved at work, I found myself in a familiar place and contemplated quitting, again. There was an unmistakable void in my life. I found myself questioning everything.

Do I retreat? Do I embrace the moment and seize the career opportunities that are right in front of me? Do I put in for a temporary leave of absence?

And then I asked myself, "How would my grandfather handle this? Would he quit? Would he ask for a leave of absence to wallow in self pity?"

My grandfather served in World War II and witnessed the deaths of many of his friends. Never in his life did he think that giving up was an option, even in the most dire circumstances. That was not only the way he lived his life but what he taught others to do, including me.

One of his great passions was baseball. He eventually would turn his love and understanding of the game into a way of giving back to the community. His passion and commitment provided a means to help keep young kids out of trouble. He volunteered his time coaching and managing a baseball team made up of troubled kids and gang members. Although I didn't fit the profile of the other kids on the team, he asked me to play on his team the summer before my freshman year of high school. When I accepted, he was thrilled. Playing on his team provided me with an exclusive glimpse into how he inspired those kids to see their potential. In turn, he helped me to see my own potential as well as understand the consequences of not taking advantage of opportunities that could improve my life. One thing I will remember forever was the respect that the team members, most of whom disdained authority, had for my grandfather. Like me, they also admired, feared and were inspired by him.

Many of my former team-mates attended grandfather's funeral. In addition to condolences, several of them expressed their gratitude for the positive affect he had had on their lives. Some went so far as to say that grandfather had saved their lives. And it didn't matter how big or tough they had grown, all of them cried as they reminisced about him.For them, he was the father and role-model that they had never had.

It didn't take me long to realize how my grandfather would have handled the same situation I now faced. I took a detailed inventory of my situation and realized I couldn't let him down. He had taught me better than that. I thought about all of those kids he had helped and inspired in the community, and I likened it to my situation with the foster kids. How could I look at myself if I walked away? My career, my success or even my failure wasn't just my own. It also affected those who looked up to me and had found inspiration in what I had accomplished up to this point. Ceasar's passing reminded me of the foster kids who had nothing, and how Billy and his siblings looked up to me for guidance. My grandfather's passing brought everything else into proper and clear perspective. In my heart and soul, I felt that if I gave up, I would not only be letting my family, friends, myself and the foster kids down, I also would be dishonoring my grandfather's memory and everything for which he stood.

From the moment I joined Allergan, as a young intern to full-time employee, I had thought success was synonymous with being #1 in sales. That idea consumed me. I had lost touch with the part of me that was real and pure. I had lost sight of what my grandfather saw in me since I was a little boy – unlimited potential. The potential he spoke of had less to do with specific skills in one area or another. It was about being true to who you are: living your life with integrity and without false air; eliminating your ego from decisions, and fully leveraging the unique gifts and talents you possessed. He always told me, "Be the best Ja Marr Brown you can be."

My grandfather was gone, but what he left me was the idea that I had the innate potential to positively change people's lives. If I was to ever achieve perennial success and live the kind of life that would have made my grandfather proud, I'd have to finally let go of my selfish, self-centered ego. I would need to embrace the potential that would make me the person my grandfather had envisioned.

A Reflection of My Grandfather

I revisited the site where my grandfather had been buried only three days before. I didn't quite know what to say, so I began with an apology.

I sat down on the lawn beside my grandfather's headstone,

and for the next hour, I came clean about setbacks, failures and how I had been slowly transforming my life by grasping my ultimate potential. I talked about my recent triumphs and all of the lessons I had learned in my journey so far. I closed things by saying how I would follow the path he had set me on when I was a little boy. I would make a difference in the lives of others the way he had done and the way he had taught me to do.

> *I had been accumulating the* How *behind selling and was now beginning to understand the true nature and power of the* Why.

Driving back home, I felt a peace and sense of purpose I thought I had lost. What could have been the saddest period of my life wound up serving as a catapult for leaping into the next phase of my journey. I had been accumulating the *How* behind selling and was now beginning to understand the true nature and power of the *Why*.

I was intent on becoming more than a sales professional that my grandfather would be proud of, but I was focused on turning my life into a reflection of what my grandfather had stood for.

STEP 18: Tapping Into Your Potential

A. Who, in your life, sees you bigger and better than you do yourself? What kind of potential do they see in you?

_____

_____

_____

B. How does the belief someone else has in you affect your performance as a sales professional? Are you overwhelmed by the pressure and expectations they have of you, or does it inspire you it to improve your performance?

_____

_____

_____

C. What level of potential do you see in yourself as a sales professional? Are you achieving that potential or wasting it?

_____

_____

_____

D. What actions can you take, from this moment on, to allow you to fulfill your potential and achieve perennial success in sales?

_____

_____

_____

Reminder ➜ Be sure to visit www.WhatsYourSalesStory.com/workbookcompanion to download the companion workbook. While at our site don't forget to share your sales story and check out the latest tips and techniques designed to help you become a perennial sales performer.

CHAPTER 12
In the Service of Others

"When you change the way you look at things,
the things you look at change."

~ Dr. Wayne Dyer ~

My perspective on life and career, along with my overall focus, was strengthened after my grandfather's passing, coupled with the lessons I learned from Ceasar's death. I returned to work feeling that I was right where I needed to be as we headed into the final months of the year.

My first week back, I had a scheduled sales call with Dr. Clark. Walking through the busy waiting room, I noticed another pharmaceutical rep at the front desk and overheard his brief interaction with the staff. Like me, months earlier, he didn't engage in any small talk or greet any of them by name. And much like me, months earlier, he was given a cold welcome and told to have a seat and wait for the doctor. The similarities were unmistakable, and I wondered if his journey would be as arduous.

Reaching the front desk, I received a warm and inviting welcome by the staff as I called them out by name and re-visited a few things we had discussed the last time I was in the office. They invited me to come to the back of the office and wait for Dr. Clark to finish with a patient.

I looked down the hallway and noticed that Dr. Clark had just walked out of a patient room. He was accompanied by an elderly African American woman who appeared to be in her late 70's. I could see that she was asking him a question, because they both stopped and were talking to each other.

While I saw the patient, my true focus was on my upcoming presentation for Dr. Clark. Even though my rapport and market share him had significantly grown, there remained crucial areas we needed to cover as we moved forward. I also felt there were ways I could even increase the business I had recently secured with him.

I'm Going Blind

I glanced at my watch and figured Dr. Clark should be wrapping up with the patient. When I shifted my focus back, I noticed a change in the interaction between them. His customarily warm, friendly and inviting demeanor with his patients had given way to a more serious look and tone. There was something different about this exchange they were having.

The little-old-lady had started to cry. I saw Dr. Clark put his arm around her. He seemed to be saying some comforting words to her. Then, Dr. Clark and the patient looked up and saw me standing down the hallway. They exchanged a few more words and then he motioned for the woman to walk over to me.

The little-old-lady made her way down the hall, heading in my direction. "This can't be good," I said to myself. I had no idea why Dr. Clark would suggest she come talk to me, but I was not prepared to interact with a patient today and did not want to be distracted from my task at hand. I turned away from her, hoping she would pass me by. Instead, I felt a slight nudge on my arm.

"Hello?"

I reluctantly turned around to find her standing in front of me, eyes were still red and moist from crying.

"I asked Dr. Clark if I could talk with you," she politely explained.

I didn't come to Dr. Clark's office to speak with patients and thought to myself, "Oh no, what is this all about? And, what in the world could she want from me?"

I smiled and pretended that I didn't hear her. Then, I turned to a staff member and asked if Dr. Clark was ready to see me.

When I turned back around, the little-old-lady was still standing there, but she had moved closer to me. I didn't quite know what to make of this and figured I could, at least, see what she wants.

"Is there something I can help you with, ma'am," I politely asked. She proceeded to tell me that she had glaucoma and Dr. Clark told her that I sold one of the medications she was taking. My initial reaction was positive as I equated her use of our product with my successful efforts to get Dr. Clark to write prescriptions for it.

"I'm sorry to hear about your glaucoma. How is the product working for you?" I glanced over her head and in the direction of where Dr. Clark was standing, only a few feet down the hallway. At first, I didn't hear her response. I assumed her answer about the product would be the same that I had learned during all of those hours studying it. Of course she was going to say it was great.

Instead of providing a testimonial for this great product, however, she informed me that she was blind in one eye and had barely 50% sight in her other eye. Needless to say, she now had my full, undivided attention.

I was dumbfounded by her condition and asked, "How was that possible? Our products are the best medications on the market." She told me that it was not due to the medicine. And then she asked me the strangest thing.

"Will you accompany me to the window?" I followed her over to the window and she pointed to a taxi cab in the parking lot.

"Young man, that's my taxi. I can't drive, and I am on a fixed income. My choices for what I can spend my money on are extremely limited. The reason I am going blind isn't because of your products; it's because I did not really understand glaucoma and how it could be treated. In the last couple of years, I missed most of my scheduled appointments with Dr. Clark, because I did not realize the seriousness of my condition. I also could not afford all of my medications."

She reached into her purse and took out a plastic sandwich bag filled with several different colored pills. She went on to tell me about her other health issues and the prescribed medications. "Your product would have helped me, but I honestly did not take my condition as seriously as I should have. In addition, there were times that I couldn't afford to have all of my prescriptions filled and usually it was my glaucoma medication that was sacrificed." she explained.

I thought about all of the calls I had made on physicians since joining Allergan, and I realized that this was the first, real interaction I had had with a patient. Sure I had passed hundreds of them over the last two-years, coming and going. I would casually say hi or asked how their day was going. I was so consumed by my own desires and focused on making the sale that I failed to see the most important part of the sales equation – actual patients who use my products.

> *"No matter what you do with your career, please do not forget about little-old-ladies like me."*

Out of my comfort zone and not sure what to say, I felt a mixture of both shock and sadness. On one hand, I was totally shocked that a woman, who desperately needed our product, found it unaffordable and did not understand her disease. On the other hand, I was saddened and devastated by this woman's story and her condition.

"Young man, I can tell by your eyes that you are a genuinely caring person. You will be successful, and I'm sure you will lead a good life. All I ask is that you do me one favor."

At first I was a little nervous to ask what this favor could be, but I put aside my insecurities and asked.

"No matter what you do with your career, please do not forget about little-old-ladies like me." She smiled and gently touched my arm and then gingerly moved across the lobby, out the front door.

Stunned and emotionally touched by this encounter, I was unable to move. While I knew there wasn't much I could do to help her situation, the realization that I could help others swept over me.

While I was present enough to recognize a profound shift in my consciousness, I also was removed from the activities around me. So much so that I didn't even hear Dr. Clark calling out my name only a few feet away.

After a moment, I turned around and saw him reviewing a patient chart. He looked up at me and before he could say anything, I said, "Thank you."

Bigger Than Me

The brief encounter with the little-old-lady completely changed my life and career. I am sure she could not have imagined the magnitude of her request for me not to forget her or others like her.

All of the training at Allergan, from the hours of role playing and studying clinical trials, to reading sales books and surviving my trials and tribulations, would not compare to the eye-opening lesson that had just been levied on me. My journey had brought me to this point, and whether my purpose had found me, or I had discovered it, one thing was unmistakably clear: I had discovered the final piece of my *Why!*

...once a salesperson is out in the field, and they're trying to survive, the customer is seen more as a means to an end than as a person with a unique story.

The personal side of my Why had been clarified and reinforced after my grandfather and Ceaser passed. But I had yet to fully grasp the final piece of the sales puzzle. You'd think it would have been obvious with the whole, "customer is king," adage that seems to be at the heart of all sales training and philosophy. While that may be true, rarely is the Why discussed and developed in sales training. The reality is that when a salesperson is out in the field trying to survive, the customer is seen more as a means to an end than as a person with a unique story.

My activities in sales had been solely driven by the need to service my own self-interests. It always was about me. Although I understood the importance of placing the spotlight on the doctors and their staff, until my little-old-lady encounter, patients were just people I passed on my way in to see the doctors. Now, I knew that their stories were important, too.

Leaving Dr. Clark's office, I actually took a real inventory of the people sitting in the waiting room. Looking from face to face, I couldn't help but wonder what their stories were, like the man on the breathing machine or the woman in the wheel chair. How had they managed to get there? Were they like the elderly woman who had to take a taxi cab? What was it that put them in the position they are in, now? How are their ailments affecting their quality of life?

Then, my eyes fell on a woman in her early 20's, sitting next to an elderly woman. I heard her ask, "Grandma, what's your social security number?" She was in the midst of filling out some forms for her grandmother, and I had to wonder what she was sacrificing in her own life to be here and help her grandmother. And what if she wasn't able to help? How would that elderly woman have gotten there and to receive medical attention?

I no longer cared about rankings, commission checks or being #1... my heart was ablaze with an unrelenting drive to help people such as that little-old-lady.

The pharmaceutical rep I had noticed earlier was still in the waiting room. Like me at one point in my career, he was oblivious to the patients around him. With an intent look on his face, he zipped through e-mails and text messages on a cell phone. I could tell he either was preparing for his call with Dr. Clark or preparing for future calls. If he only knew just how important the individual stories of the patients were to the success of his career. I also wondered why he wasn't up and chatting with the office staff. More than likely, he didn't even know their names, let alone a single thing about them on a personal level.

It was a revelation! Before I had met the little-old-lady, who asked me not to forget people like her, the chairs in the waiting room could just as well have been empty. I honestly didn't see the people sitting in them. I knew from that moment on, I never would breeze through another patient waiting room, unaware.

I wanted to know their stories: Not because I saw this as a way to boost my sales, I genuinely cared about their stories and was eager to listen and apply what I learned from them.

The Cloak Had Been Lifted

The cloak had been lifted, and I couldn't help but recognize the irony in past events. My entire perception of what I did for a living and who I did it for was irrevocably changed by little-old-lady who could barely see. And while she was going blind, my eyes had just been opened. No more obstructed vision, I finally could see the world I worked in.

My purpose as a sales professional had altered: I no longer cared about rankings, commission checks or being #1. From then on, my heart was ablaze with an unrelenting drive to help people such as that little-old-lady.

There was no question in my mind that a major key to success was to provide better educational materials, support patient screenings and provide extra samples for the less fortunate. I also found out that Allergan had a special program for indigent patients where they could get medications for free.

Due to my focus on selling to the doctors and being #1, I never considered the special program of any great relevance to me. After hearing the little-old-lady's story, coupled with the fact that part of my territory stretched across some of the poorest communities of LA, I went on a mission to educate my doctors and sign up as many patients that qualified for the program as I could. I also re-doubled my efforts in my work with the managed-care team to ensure that all of our drugs were covered by the key managed-care plans in my territory.

Those accomplishments turned up the volume on my excitement to visit doctors' offices. I now was able to tell my doctors that all of my products were covered, and patients who really could not afford them, would receive them free of charge.

That little-old-lady I met had asked that I never forget about her and to help others in similar situations. While we never saw each other again, her presence and what she represented continued to move me to action.

I am proud to say that not a single day has passed, since we crossed paths, that I haven't discovered ways to keep my promise to her. She has served as a never-ending reminder of what I stand for, who I work for and who I serve as a sales professional.

STEP 19: What Do You Stand For?

No matter how clear or unclear our intentions may be, everyone, including sales professionals, have a purpose. It isn't a question of whether you are driven by something, but what is that something that drives you?

Step 19 is a crucial piece to writing your own story. In fact, it is the heart of your story, both literally and figuratively. This is the part of your story where you strip away the exterior of who you are. Remove the obvious motivations such as the money, recognition, respect and awards, and be prepared to answer the following questions.

A. What do you stand for? *(Think about what you truly care about.)*

_____

_____

_____

B. Who fills the role of the "little-old-lady" in your career? *(Think in terms of the one person who symbolizes your purpose for selling. Who is it that serves as your anchor and reminder of who you are, what you stand for and, ultimately, whose life you're enriching?)*

_____

_____

_____

Reminder ➜ Be sure to visit www.WhatsYourSalesStory.com/workbookcompanion to download the companion workbook. While at our site don't forget to share your sales story and check out the latest tips and techniques designed to help you become a perennial sales performer.

CHAPTER 13
The How + The Why = The Beginning

"Live your life from your heart. Share from your heart.
And your story will touch and heal people's souls."
~ Melody Beattie ~

The most tumultuous year of my life had revealed a clearly defined vision underscored by a renewed passion and purpose. The lessons I had learned along the way culminated, reaching a crescendo with the little-old-lady in Dr. Clark's office.

I had put in hundreds of hours learning the *How's* of successful selling. It wasn't until I had painstakingly learned the *Why's* behind successful selling that I was poised to dramatically grow my career and profoundly impact the lives of the patients with our products. Applied in tandem, the *How* and the *Why* created an unstoppable force.

The Rankings

In 1998, things got off to an excellent start when the first-month's sales rankings were revealed. My position had moved from number 91 out of 98 in December of 1997 to 27 by January.

Several colleagues and managers from across our region as well as those in the corporate office called to congratulate me. During that year, I routinely would receive emails and calls about how my numbers continued to increase. Because I continued to climb in the rankings, by the middle of the year, many people at

People would ask me why my numbers were skyrocketing. I would reply by saying that I was simply helping little-old-ladies.

Allergan, including the VPS and my manager, were saying I had a great chance of reaching the #1 spot that year. Each time, I genuinely thanked them for congratulating me but ended each call by asking them not to share my rankings with me for the rest of the year. It wasn't that I was not aware of them, but I was no longer consumed or driven by the numbers.

People would ask me why my numbers were skyrocketing. I would reply by saying that I was simply helping little-old-ladies. At first, they thought I was joking. When they discovered I wasn't, they thought I was crazy. Aiming to be the #1 rep in the company, focused on making more money than everyone else, earning a trip to Hawaii, these things made sense to other reps. Focused on helping people you would most likely never talk to wasn't easily understood.

I had certainly made a monumental leap, sales-wise, but it paled in comparison to the breadth and depth of the leap I had made in my overall mindset towards being perennially successful at sales.

I could go on about how my numbers continued to skyrocket in 1998, but it really is not important. Yes, I broke sales records, and yes, I won leadership council, presidents club, Salesperson of the Year and a promotion to senior territory manager. Those things really did not matter at the time and still don't, today. I don't wear my diamond ring or hang numerous plaques and trophies on my office wall for all to see and admire. What has driven me since that chance encounter with the little-old-lady still drives me today. It is a *Relentless Pursuit of Excellence.*

All of the market share gains, accolades and business earned did not mean I was simply making more money. To me it meant that I was making a difference in the lives of patients, helping little-old-ladies.

Every End Has a Beginning

Everyone has a story to tell. From the CEO, managers, sales reps and receptionists to the janitors and cleaning crew, every company is built on the stories of the individuals who come through its doors. Their stories, whether you know them or not, shape, guide and ultimately determine the culture and success of every company.

As a salesperson, you may look to the top reps in your company and be jealous of them, revere them or be inspired by them. In some cases, you could feel all of those emotions. No matter how you look at them, if you ever wish to join their rank, and become one of the best-of-the-best, you'll want to know their stories. Their numbers only tell a portion of that story. How they got there and how they consistently achieve such a high level of success is where the truth of their success can be found.

> *Before you can understand anyone else's story, however, you must first understand yours.*

The same can be said about your customers. The level of success you have with them, and how you grow and sustain that success, is predicated by the depth of knowledge you possess about their individual stories.

Do any of the following questions keep you up at night: *How can I increase my market share? How can I grow my sales and exceed quota? How can I blow out my commission checks?*

The answers are simple. Learn and leverage your customers' stories. Listen to and apply what you learn from their stories, and you will have unlocked the code that makes them who they are. In return, you will watch your sales numbers skyrocket.

Before you can understand anyone else's story, however, you must first understand yours. I provided my story as a guide for you to uncover your own. You should already have begun to see your story through the personal story development exercises provided to you throughout the book. Now, it's a matter of applying what you have learned in the sales field and your personal life.

The Story Behind the Names

The vividness of the memories I had about my career had momentarily taken my attention off of the video. I rewound the tape to the point where I walked up on the stage. Watching myself, again, I relived the moment as if I was right there in Hawaii.

There I stood on the stage, gazing out across the audience at a sea of endless faces. Some of them I recognized, others I had never seen before. More than 400 people. Several of them were previous Salesperson-of-the-Year winners, and they stared at me, eagerly anticipating my next set of words. In those brief seconds, I retraced my steps from the days as a young, brash and unseasoned sales rookie through the lessons I had learned and how those lessons had brought me to the very stage I now stood on.

I glanced back to the names on the index card I was holding. I may have been the one standing on that stage, receiving the accolades, but those individuals, whose names were on the index card, they were the ones who carried me here. I originally planned on talking about my efforts over the past year, the percentage that my sales had increased and how I achieved the #1 position in sales.

> *The only thing I will ever take credit for is the fact that I removed my ego from the sales process and learned to truly listen to people and hear their stories.*

After arriving in Hawaii, where the event took place, I decided to throw away what I had written. Instead of the customary canned, meticulously prepared speech that speaks to the virtues of hard work and sales techniques used, I chose to tell the story behind those names on the index card.

As I stated to the audience that evening and have maintained ever since, I will never take credit for my success. What I have accomplished is because of the names on the index card. They represent many of the people you've read about in this book. They came in and out of my life, inspiring me, teaching me and guiding me to reach my full potential and turn around not just my career, but my life. Most of them did all of this without even knowing it or realizing the impact it would have on me.

But that index card I held represented so much more than just those names; it represented their stories. The only thing I will ever take credit for is the fact that I removed my ego from the sales process and learned to truly listen to people and hear their stories. I let them share their insights and their stories with me. And I applied what I learned.

STEP 20: Why Do You Sell?

A. Why do you sell? *Stretch yourself and go beyond the "money" and "recognition." For example, what does the money you earn get applied to and why? Are you applying your money to just pay the bills? If so, what happens when they're paid, now what? Are you simply surviving or are you yearning for a rich and fulfilling life?*

If so, than you can rest assured that you are selling for more than just money, recognition and ego. Consider the Why and how it is bigger than you or the accolades you may receive. Whatever it is, write it down.

_____

_____

_____

_____

_____

_____

STEP 20: Why Do You Sell? (continued)

B. If you were to combine all that you know about selling (the *HOW*) with the power of your *WHY*, what is it that you could achieve in your career? *(Answer this with the idea that there are no limits to what you can attain.)*

_____

_____

_____

_____

_____

_____

STEP 21: Tell Your Story

This is the final step in your story.

A. Now that you have developed your own story, who will you tell it to? *You may be reluctant to share your story, but think about the individuals in your life that could benefit from the inspiration and knowledge gained from your story.*

_____

_____

_____

B. When will you tell them your story?

_____

_____

_____

C. What are the key lessons from your story, and what do you want others to take away from hearing it?

_____

_____

_____

D. What is the ending of your story, and what new beginning will evolve from this?

_____

_____

_____

_____

Reminder ➜ Be sure to visit www.WhatsYourSalesStory.com/ workbookcompanion to download the companion workbook. While at our site don't forget to share your sales story and check out the latest tips and techniques designed to help you become a perennial sales performer.

The Beginning

My acceptance speech concluded, and the crowd stood in unison, applauding. I sat there, on my sofa, smiling, as the video of my acceptance speech ended.

For the past several minutes, I had watched the acceptance speech and, in my own mind, I was taken back to those tumultuous, yet career and life- altering years. The names I had read off the index card during the speech vividly reminded me of the ups and downs I had endured and overcome, including the sorrows and joy, huge disappointments, and of course, the priceless fulfillment of success.

I realized it was the right time to open up a new chapter in my story. If I were to truly fulfill my promise to that little-old-lady from and serve as an anchor and inspiration to others as my grandfather had, it was clear to me that my story had to be told. The decision to share my story, which would culminate in the book you're reading, was born that Saturday morning.

> *All stories have a beginning, middle and end. The irony is that with every end rises an opportunity for a glorious new beginning.*

"Daddy?" the voice of my daughter, Alexis, brought me out of my thoughts. "What are you doing," she asked as she walked over and hopped into my arms.

A few moments later, over a bowl of cereal, I shared the video of my acceptance speech with her. The second she saw my face, her eyes lit up, and she said, "Daddy you're on TV. You're famous."

Smiling, I said, "No honey, I won an award, because I helped people. She then asked about the index card in my hand and why I was holding it. I told her it contained names of people who are very important to me. I said they represented my *Story*. Of course, this didn't mean much to her, and she said I was silly.

Her attention and interest in the video waned, and she now was asking me to put on some cartoons. Getting up to turn the channel on the television, I looked back at Alexis. The names on the index card will forever hold a special place in my life. They were my *Why* when I didn't have one. I am forever grateful for the wisdom and lessons I learned from those who played such a pivotal role in my early sales career.

Stories are anything but predictable, especially when you are factoring in the twists and turns that come with life. But they do have a structure and framework that rarely, if ever, changes. All stories have a beginning, middle and end. The irony is that with every end rises an opportunity for a glorious, new beginning.

Watching my daughter play that morning, I was once again struck by how important the *Why* is to one's story and perennial success. Every day, I am inspired by her presence and the wondrous and limitless possibilities that lie ahead for her.

At this stage of my life, I am more driven by my legacy than career. What will I leave for my daughter? How will she come to know her father? How can I better prepare her for the challenges she will no doubt face in her life? Obviously, I cannot protect my daughter from everything, but I can use my story to illustrate the importance of not letting her ego get in the way of her success.

Before she came into my life, the little-old-lady served as my biggest *Why*. She inspired and drove me to reach new heights throughout my career. Today, my wife, Amanda, and Alexis serve as the two biggest *Whys* in my life. They are as much a part of my *Why* now, as the little-old-lady was to the success I enjoyed during my days at Allergan.

As my life has progressed, with one chapter ending and a new, even more exciting one beginning, my story continues to evolve. In fact, my own story is not only far from over, it is only just beginning.

Now, it's your turn to tell your story.

Meet Ja Marr Brown

Ja Marr Brown is the creator of The KAIZEN Way ® a revolutionary sales and management system. A highly sought after corporate sales consultant, trainer and speaker, Ja Marr is known for introducing a "reality-based" approach to sales excellence.

A highly accomplished and widely respected sales and management executive, Ja Marr has over 15 years of senior-level sales and management experience in both the pharmaceutical and medical device industries.

Ja Marr is currently District Manager for a leading medical device company, overseeing the western region's sales activities. Prior to that Ja Marr enjoyed a 13 year successful career at Allergan Pharmaceuticals, one of the most respected pharmaceutical companies in the world.

A former Student Body President and graduate of Whittier College, Ja Marr received his degree in Business with an emphasis in marketing. While in college, Ja Marr applied for and was accepted into the prestigious INROADS internship program where he would later be named Alumnus of the Year and Supervisor of the Year.

Through the INROADS program, Ja Marr was selected as Allergan's first summer intern. Upon graduation, Allergan offered Ja Marr a full time sales position. He would find himself in the Los Angeles area, which was the lowest ranked territory in the country at the time. Over the course of two and a half years, he was able to move the territory from last in the country to first and received the prestigious Salesperson of the Year award in 1998.

During the course of the next eight years Ja Marr would rise to even loftier heights as he developed a new selling system for Allergan and trained all of Allergan's 300 person sales force. He also oversaw the marketing initiatives for one of Allergan's most successful product launches. Ja Marr finished his career at Allergan by transforming a last placed sales team into the #1 sales team in the nation and being promoted to Regional Sales Director, becoming one of the youngest individuals to ever hold that position.

Ja Marr lives in Orange County with his wife and daughter.

To you it's more than just another event. So hire more than just another speaker.

Whether you're a sales executive looking at training for your sales force, a seasoned meeting planner or program director looking for a top flight keynote speaker, you know that locating speakers who can relate to, inspire and be memorable is easier said than done...until now.

Ja Marr Brown's reality based approach to sales and sales management, coupled with his dynamic, thought provoking and engaging style captivates audiences of all sizes.

His innate ability to relate to his audience makes it easy for audience members, no matter their experience level or career goals, to begin successfully applying Ja Marr's strategies and techniques in their lives right away, in some cases, the very same day.

Audiences Love Ja Marr's Reality Based Keynotes

Known for his inspirational and real life stories, Ja Marr refers to his brand of speaking as "reality based presentations". Rather than rely on worn out, clichéd analogies or out of date sales lessons, Ja Marr brings a brand of realism to the topics of sales and management rarely seen from today's professional speakers.

It's Time to Captivate Your Audience

Enhance your next meeting, conference, or convention with an expert speaker who will not only make you look good but will deliver long-term value to your audience.

To schedule a meeting with Ja Marr to discuss having him as your keynote speaker please email info@whatsyoursalesstory.com.

www.WhatsYourSalesStory.com

Pick up where the book leaves off with the *What's Your Sales Story?* blog. Visit www.WhatsYourSalesStory.com and receive timely articles, tips and insights on achieving sales excellence.